T3-BRL-546

Wholeness
and
Holiness

Wholeness and Holiness

A Christian Response to Human Suffering

A Theology of Health Care Ministry

Cornelius J. van der Poel, C.S.Sp.

SHEED & WARD
Franklin, Wisconsin

As an apostolate of the Priests of the Sacred Heart, a Catholic religious order, the mission of Sheed & Ward is to publish books of contemporary impact and enduring merit in Catholic Christian thought and action. The books published, however, reflect the opinion of their authors and are not meant to represent the official position of the Priests of the Sacred Heart.

1999

BX
2347.8
.S5
P65
1999

Sheed & Ward
7373 South Lovers Lane Road
Franklin, Wisconsin 53132
1-800-558-0580

Copyright © 1999 by Cornelius J. van der Poel

All rights reserved. No part of this book may be reproduced, stored in a retrieval system, or transmitted in any form or by any means—electronic, mechanical, photocopying, recording, or otherwise—without the written permission of Sheed & Ward.

Printed in the United States of America

Cover and interior design: Scott Wannemuehler, GrafixStudio, Inc.

Library of Congress Cataloging-in-Publication Data

Poel, Cornelius J. van der, 1921–
    Wholeness and holiness : a Christian response to human suffering / Cornelius J. van der Poel.
        p.   cm.
    ISBN 1-58051-054-X
    1. Church work with the sick.   2. Pastoral medicine—Catholic Church.   3. Suffering—Religious aspects—Catholic Church.
    I. Title
    BX2347.8.S5P85   1999
    259′ .4—dc21   98-52525
                                                          CIP

1 2 3 4 5 / 02 01 00 99

Table of Contents

Acknowledgments

I want to express my most sincere thanks to the many people who have in any way contributed to the writing of this book: In the very first place my students in the Health Care Ministry programs at Duquesne University in Pittsburgh and at Barry University in Miami. Their constructive critique and continued encouragement greatly contributed to the shape and content of this work. A special word of thanks also to David Kelly, Ph.D., Marilyn Schaub, Ph.D., and James Hanigan, Ph.D., at Duquesne University; Rev. John O'Grady, S.T.D., S.S.D., and Edward Sunshine, Ph.D., at Barry University for their keen interest and valuable advice.

Preface

"Health care ministry" is an expression with a variety of meanings. For some people it means the concern for the spiritual care of patients in hospitals. For Catholics it often means to administer the sacraments of the Eucharist and Anointing to the sick and the dying. Others understand health care ministry as any form of involvement with health care delivery. Some people classify health care ministry as a separate profession among the "service" areas of human relationships, while others consider it as a particular quality in any profession that deals with the concern for the sick. Some people again see health care ministry as a profession in its own right, or they call any involvement in health care delivery a form of health care ministry. Therefore, a clear understanding of its *meaning* is necessary for the study of a theology of health care ministry.

Health care ministry is for me both a quality and a profession. It is *a quality* in so far as every professional who works with the sick is called to alleviate a sick person's pain or discomfort. Their professionalism is one of the contributing factors that assist sick persons to improve their life and activity, or to find a new balance that makes life in its present condition more livable. *Every professional relationship with patients has an element of service that quite accurately may be understood as a ministerial quality.*

Health care ministry is also *a profession in its own right*. Human life is by nature a process of integration in which the current physical, psychological, and spiritual abilities of an individual must blend together into the best harmonious unity that can be achieved in the present circumstances. Illness is a disharmony in either the physical, psychological, or spiritual dimensions of a person, or in all of them. A disharmony in any of these human dimensions causes an imbalance in the total person. *Health care ministry as profession focuses on restoring a proper balance.* This ministry is a healing function which has a broader scope than the service element inherent in any individual branch of health care delivery, such as nursing or physiotherapy. Its focus is human wholeness, but it cannot fully and effectively function without other professions.

Health care ministry is normally seen as a form of spiritual care. This is correct, provided that spirituality is not understood as an independent quality alongside other qualities in human life. Spirituality is rather a quality that gives unity and direction to life itself. It is the human acceptance of God's presence with us and God's influence on everyday existence. Spirituality is a description of the manner in which an individual responds to the constant invitation to serve God (or to become what God asks him or her to be).

From this point of view, health care ministry is indeed a profession which is not only related to spiritual life, but has in itself a redemptive quality. Its immediate concern is the restoration of the individual's personal balance and integrity at this time of disharmony. It is a direct contribution to the patient's peace of mind, physical comfort, and friendship with God. This friendship with God is redemptive. It is the ability to love God unconditionally. Genuine health care ministry that contributes to surrender and peace has a redemptive power.

The approach to this form of ministry is closely related to the religious denomination to which a patient belongs. Therefore, health care ministry is usually considered to be a concern of the Churches. This is only partially accurate because health care ministry deals with human wholeness rather than exclusively with spiritual perspectives. It is, therefore, as much a concern of the health care facility and of the health care profession in general. Health care ministry as a separate profession integrates the physical, psychological, and spiritual dimensions of the health care delivery into a holistic human concern.

In the present study I intend to focus primarily on health care ministry as a profession and as a supportive and integrative quality in health care professionalism. It is important to remember that health care ministry is not the prerogative of clergy or religious. It is a charge that is built into human nature and that the Scriptures, in particular the gospels, present as a mandate to the whole religious, human, and Christian community.

What is presented in the following pages is, therefore, not intended for a few professionals but for anyone who wants to respond to the mandates of human life and to the scriptural message of healing placed upon all. A deeper understanding of the total message will help believers to respond more effectively to God's call for healing and redemption (as wholeness and redemption).

Illness, even if
it seems to be a
physical illness only,
upsets the proper
balance in the total
person, including
the balance in his
or her relationships
with others and often
in relationship with
God.

CHAPTER ONE

Health Care Ministry:
A Human and Christian Task

CREATION CALLS FOR MINISTRY

Health care ministry is an active concern for wholeness and well-being in people who are physically or emotionally ill. Ministry, or supportive concern and assistance, is called for by the human condition itself when an individual is disabled or has significant difficulty dealing with life and its responsibilities. Human wholeness is achieved when there is an appropriate balance between the physical, psychological, or emotional and spiritual dimensions in an individual. Illness, even if it seems to be a physical illness only, upsets the proper balance in the total person, including the balance in his or her relationships with others and often in relationship with God. This imbalance is usually painful and causes suffering. Health care ministry responds to this imbalance and, therefore, it does not simply respond to pain caused by an external illness. It responds to the total person.

Interpersonal relationships are not a luxury in human life that can be ignored at whim. They are essential to human existence. We are all aware of the enormous influence that early relationships have upon the formation of the personality. We know how isolation can change a person. In the following discussions I want to reflect on the interpersonal nature of human existence.

I accept that human life is more than physical existence and psychological interaction. It also has a spiritual dimension that gives goal and direction to the individual and society. This spiritual perspective is part of the true understanding of the human condition. I start from the premise that *the human being is created in the image of God.*

The acceptance that we are created includes necessarily that we exist in interpersonal relationships. Creation is a communication of existence. It presupposes interaction between a giver and a receiver, it means dependence, it means relationship. In other words, human beings cannot be totally themselves in complete isolation. This is important for our understanding of ministry. Interhuman concern belongs to human nature. We cannot develop into healthy and balanced individuals without supportive assistance from others: *others must minister to us.* Ministry is not a "do-goodery," it has its own proper place within the arena of normal human life and fulfillment.

Creation as Interhuman Relationship[1]

Creation is not fully described in the usual definition of "making something out of nothing." I rather describe it as *"the communication and sharing of the deepest layers of one's own being for the existence, growth, and development of another."* In ordinary human terminology we often speak about creative art or creative thinking. What we mean, then, is that a deep feeling and ability of an individual is translated into a new and independent existence apart from the artist. In this process of translation, the artist does not lose his feelings. On the contrary, while these inner feelings receive an independent external existence, the inner self and feelings are enriched and deepened. Experts in the field will have no difficulty recognizing the difference between the paintings of Rembrandt and Van Gogh. Both artists had their own personality and put their own personal imprint on the expression of their feelings. Time and culture may influence artistic expressions and lead to certain similarities so that we can legitimately speak of different schools of art and painting, but personal characteristics remain always visible.

The incorporation of the life and emotions of one person into another shows even clearer when we reflect on the creative work of composers and musicians. A person who plays the piano can reproduce the music and feelings of the composer. Let us say that the pianist plays a symphony of Bach. If the pianist is an expert, anyone can recognize Bach's style and music. At the same time, the personality, the expertise, and the style of the pianist are revealed in the presentation. An expert reproduction displays the blending of artist and composer. This unity between the musician and the composer is so strong that it becomes impossible to say where the one stops and the other begins. The best way to explain this is to say that Bach is alive through the expertise and personality of the musician.

These two steps, (1) the recognition that existence is a special manifestation of the inner depth of the maker, and (2) the acceptance that this new existence (the reproduction of Bach) is a blending of the inner person of the composer and the feelings of the artist, give us a clearer understanding of the meaning of creation. In creation God manifests the inner depth of his own being. He expresses himself. He communicates his own life and shares it with the creatures. St. Thomas Aquinas points out that every existence is a certain participation in God's own being (*Summa Theologica* I, 44). This has a particular meaning in the creation of the human being who is made in the image and likeness of God (*Summa Theologica* II–II, Prol.). Image and likeness cannot be explained by concepts of picture image or sound reproduction. Image and likeness means a sharing in the life of God. The Gospel of St. John points this out where Jesus calls himself the true vine and his disciples the branches (Jn. 15:5). Jesus repeats this in the priestly prayer when he says:

> Father, may they be one in us, as you are in me and I am in you.... With me in them and you in me may they be so completely one that the world will realize that it was you who sent me ... (Jn. 17:21–23).

In other words, those who believe in God will live by the life of God.

Concern for the well-being of others lies at the heart of Jesus' teaching. In answer to the questions of the disciples of John the Baptizer whether he was the Messiah, Jesus (paraphrasing the prophet Isaiah in 35:5) said:

> Go and tell John what you hear and see:
> The blind see again and the lame walk,
> lepers are cleansed and the deaf hear,
> and the dead are raised to life and
> the good news is proclaimed to the poor ...
> (Mt. 11:5).

John points out that the central characteristic of the messianic era is a constructive, supportive, and creative relationship. The same doctrine is presented in the narrative of the final judgment (referring to the scriptural teaching of Tobit 4:16 and Job 31:17): "I was hungry and you gave me food; I was thirsty and you gave me drink, a stranger and you welcomed me" (Mt. 25:35–45). The message is the same. A constructive interhuman relationship is the external manifestation of the internal and real relationship with God.

Reflecting on this teaching, it becomes clear that the human being who is created in the image of God and shares in the life of God can be fully human only when his or her life reflects the life of God, or translates the life of God into a visible reality. Consequently, interhuman relationships are fully human only when they are a constructive, supportive, creative, and redemptive exchange in which each individual contributes to the growth and development of others. Such contributions are, in the true sense of the word, *ministries*. They are a service that one person extends to another for the benefit of the receiver, but they are simultaneously a contribution to the development of the one who renders the service. The concern for the wholeness of others is a necessity for personal growth. This demand for mutual concern flows forth from the nature of being human, and although it refers to any form of human growth, it has a special meaning in the human relationship with the sick where human insufficiency is most evident, where personal surrender is needed, and where supportive and loving presence is indispensable. Human growth and wholeness is achieved in this mutuality of exchange, which is the human expression of God's creative presence.

Constructive mutual help and support belong to human life. Something is lacking in the wholeness of the individual if this giving and receiving does not take place. In other words, ministry is part of human life.

This brief reflection on the human condition as manifestation of God's creative love shows us that:

> Ministry is a personal involvement of a believing person in the physical, emotional, and spiritual well-being of others for the good of giver and receiver.

> Ministry is not an activity of one individual to another in isolation. It is an activity in which the community comes to wholeness through the activity of one individual to another who both are members and representatives of the community.

> Ministry is an enabling function in which the best of one individual calls forth and enables the best in the life of another and thus contributes to the growth of individual and community.

THE SCRIPTURES INVITE US TO MINISTRY

The Scriptures tell us about the relationship between God and humanity and about the relationship of human beings among themselves. The Scriptures are God's self-revelation, but they also communicate what expectations God has placed upon humanity. This revelation of God's actions and goals found its fulfillment in Christ who by his life and teaching showed humanity how to serve the Father in one another. The ministry that is inherent to the human condition was lived by Christ, it was understood and practiced by the apostles, and it spread throughout the world under the inspiration of the Spirit. The Scriptures show us how (1) Christ "modeled" ministry, (2) the apostles "preached" it, and (3) it spread under the "inspiration" of the Holy Spirit.

Christ, the Model of Ministry

Concerns for the sick and for the well-being of all people are the clearest examples of ministry in the life of Jesus. They manifest his compassion for the afflicted. He came to bring "wholeness" to individuals and to the human community. However, Jesus did not come as a mere individual. He came as a representative or as the incorporation of all humanity. He was God in human *nature.* The life of Christ highlights the original goal and dignity of human existence. In Christ human nature itself received the potential to share in the divine life. In this way Christ became the fullness of humanity as a whole as well as of every individual. Consequently, the task that he fulfilled was not a task in isolation. It was a task to be shared by all who were to share in his life. Accepting Christ is also accepting the life and task he lived for us and with us. All humanity is called to take part in this task, but it is in particular the task of those who have freely accepted to believe in him. His own life and teaching show the qualities and relationships that he wants to be characteristic of his disciples.

Jesus expects that his followers will express in their life human compassion and support for those who are in need. They must bring alleviation and consolation to the hungry and the thirsty, to the sick and to prisoners, because "what you have done to any of my brethren, you have done to me" (Mt. 25:40). Discipleship of Christ seems impossible without active involvement for the sake of others.

Serving presence may not become an authoritarian imposition. In Luke 22:24–27 Jesus warns: "The greatest among you must behave as if he were the youngest, and the leader as if he were the one who serves." The meaning is obvious. Leadership in the community may not be authoritarian or imposing; it must be supportive. Similarly, the service given to others may not lead to subjection; it may not diminish the dignity of anyone. It should rather lead to freedom and to the full development of those who are served.

At the time of his ascension, Jesus sent his apostles out into the world to fulfill his mission. He prefaced this act of commissioning with the words: "All authority in heaven and on earth has been given to me" (Mt. 28:18). But this, too, is not intended as an authority to impose doctrine or behavior. Rather he commands them to teach all nations and to observe what he had taught them earlier (Mt. 28:19–20).

St. Paul highlights another dimension of the nature of service. He stresses a corporate ministry. The image of the body signifies the relationship between the community of the Church and Christ (1 Cor. 12:12–30). This image presents the life and message of Christ as the source of life for the Church. This same doctrine also indicates the mutual responsibility of the members and the utilization of one's individual abilities for the good of the community. When Paul speaks about the diversity of gifts which the Spirit bestows on the believers (1 Cor. 12:4–11), he points out that these gifts are for the good of the community and not primarily for the benefit of the individual. (See 1 Cor. 12:7.)

Humanity is called to live the life of God, but no individual can have or live all the divine qualities. Human beings are interdependent. The complementarity and dove-tailing of qualities and gifts constitute relationships and create community. Therefore, the purpose of special gifts is the building of community. To receive special gifts is a call to personal involvement and to exercise one's responsibility in the building up of the society (cf., 1 Cor. 12:4–11; Eph. 4:11–12; Rom. 12:6–8). Every individual has the responsibility to use his or her gifts for the good of others. Each individual must contribute to the spiritual well-being (wholeness) of all. The life of Jesus shows this form of dedication in which personal development and the development of the community blend into one expression of service to God and neighbor. In Jesus we see this blending of personal growth and development of the community in one human expression.

The Teaching of the Apostles and of the Early Church

Jesus commissioned his apostles to bring his teaching to all humankind. Their original involvement was preaching as well as caring for those who were in need. The pressure resulting from the increased numbers of followers made it necessary to divide their tasks into several parts. "It would not be right for us to neglect the word of God so as to give out food"(Acts 6:2). They established a separate form of ministry that transferred a part of their activity to the responsibility of people chosen by the community from the community. They established a community involvement different from but complementary to the primary charge of the apostles. Thus we see a ministry performed under the authority of the apostles but carried out by the community. The collaboration between these two branches constitutes the wholeness of ministry.

Paul mentioned several individuals who worked with him in various communities, for example, Clement who worked at Philippi (Ph. 4:3), and the Stephanas family who supported the Church in Corinth (1 Cor. 15:15). These persons seem not to belong to the "apostolic institution or hierarchy" but their "vocation as Christians" seems to qualify them for their special tasks. Peter called to life the woman, Tabitha, (Acts 9:36), "who never tired of doing good or giving charity." Her involvement was a response to her Christian vocation.

In the course of the centuries, the Church's ministry became strongly clericalized. Almost all activities that related to the Church and to the spiritual well-being of the faithful were either done by clergy or by people under their immediate supervision. The involvement of the lay community was mostly limited to the performance of corporeal and spiritual works of mercy, almost entirely under clergy supervision, but they had no official status. They were considered the "arm and hand" of the clergy.

Toward the early part of the 20th century, "Catholic Action" came to the foreground. An official "Canonical Mission" was often granted to those persons who wanted to join in the "apostolate of the hierarchy." There was no such thing as an apostolate of the laity. The community at large did not have an authentic role or recognition.

Vatican Council II sees the Church as the People of God which, as community, is responsible for its well-being and progress. Certain functions are entrusted to specific persons either through assignment or because of ordination. However, the overall functioning of the Christian community is presented as the rightful involvement of all the members. Consequently, although lay people can be constituted as helpers of the clergy in certain functions related to the ministerial priesthood or to the governing functions in the community, they also have, by right, their own responsibilities. They have the right to be involved and to participate in the life and activity of the Church by nature of their membership through Baptism and not merely because of a special delegation by the hierarchy.

The Code of Canon Law summarizes the teaching of Vatican Council II in canon 204 paragraph 1, which defines the faithful as: "those who, inasmuch as they have been incorporated in Christ through baptism, have been constituted as the people of God . . . " Then, in canon 205, the Code states that persons are fully in communion with the Catholic Church when they are joined with Christ in the visible structure of the Church by the bonds of profession of faith, of the sacraments, and of ecclesiastical governance. In subsequent canons the Code gives a list of the rights that belong to the lay people by nature of their membership in the Church. In doing so the Code brings together the teachings of such Council documents as *Lumen gentium* (LG) Chapter IV (nos. 30–38), *Apostolicam actuositatem* (AA), particularly nos. 2–4, 9–14, and *Gaudium et spes* (GS), particularly nos. 33–39 and all of Part II.

The rights of lay people within the Church do not place them in opposition to the hierarchy. The final responsibility for the maintenance of the teaching of Christ and for the interpretation of revelation rests with the authority that Jesus instituted. But this authority does not act on its own without the community of the faithful. The Spirit speaks and reveals God's love to the Church as a whole, which includes the laity as well as the hierarchy. While it is the responsibility of the teaching authority to formulate and preserve the content of faith and doctrine, it is also the responsibility of the same authority to lead and to inspire the people at large to an ever greater participation in the search for the meaning and role of Christ's message in the life of contemporary society. *We may say that the Church will be alive only to the extent that the laity (the total community of believers) is actively involved with and concerned about the well-being of the total Church.* The hierarchy may not exclude or paralyze the laity, nor can the laity disregard the hierarchy.

It is important to keep in mind that, in the teaching of Vatican Council II, the laity is not merely a help to the hierarchy when there is a lack of priests. The laity is a source of apostolic activity in its own right (canon 216). They have, therefore, a right and responsibility to be engaged in the apostolate also when there is an abundance of priests. This teaching has been explicitly stated in a letter of the West German Bishops' Conference of March 2, 1977: *"Zur Ordung der Pastoralen Dienste"* (n. 1, 1. 1, p. 6). They state that it is the task of the community not only to receive pastoral care, but also to participate actively in the apostolic mission of the Church (n. 3.2, p. 15).

Vatican Council II understands ministry in a very broad way, which includes sacramental ministry as well as ministry of leadership and all other Christian services. It allows for "institutionalized" ministry, (ordained ministry and ministry instituted by the hierarchy and serving under its supervision) as well as "non-ordained" ministry, which is not necessarily performed in the name of the hierarchy. Working with youth or as a hospital chaplain can rightly be called special ministries. The hierarchy, however, has the right to select certain forms of non-ordained ministry and constitute them as an extension of its own official ministry. These specially selected ministries are mostly related to public worship, such as lector and acolyte (cf., *Apostolicam actuositatem* and *Gaudium et spes,* passim). The hierarchy must inspire and encourage lay ministries; it may evaluate them but may not stand in their way.

The Action of the Holy Spirit

Earlier I have described ministry as an *involvement for the spiritual well-being of others.* It is a sharing in the mission of the Church, or in the mission of sanctification. The Holy Spirit is the source of all sanctification. Any form of true ministry, therefore, must be an expression of the self-communication of the Spirit to humanity. Jesus promised another Advocate who would be sent by the Father to instruct the apostles in everything (cf., Jn. 14:26; 15:26). The Spirit bestows his gifts for the good of the community (cf., 1 Cor. 12:4–30), and those who receive these gifts are responsible for using them for the growth and support of others. Every true ministry has a spiritual dimension or motivation. Ministry cannot be reduced to "just another job," nor can every human occupation on its own merit be considered as a "ministry." *Human activity becomes ministry when it is a (conscious and intended) contribution and assistance to humanity in its relationship to God.*

In the above discussions the concept of ministry remains rather broad and can be applied to any form of physical and emotional involvement of the People of God for the spiritual well-being of the community. It is an involvement that flows forth from being members of the community and, within certain limitations, it is the right and responsibility of all because all are members of the same body, living from the same source of life and guided by the same Spirit.

The word "pastoral," which is frequently added to the word ministry, indicates a qualifying and descriptive dimension.

The exact meaning of "pastoral" is nowhere defined, but, in ecclesiastical writings, it seems always to include a concerned involvement for the good of others beyond the scope of law or its implementation. We see this expressed in the "Instruction on the Proper Implementation of the Constitution on Sacred Liturgy" *Inter Oecumenici* of Sept. 26, 1964, n. 5. This document states that the Constitution on Sacred Liturgy does not aim merely and exclusively at a change in rites and texts. It aims at spiritual formation and must lead to pastoral activity.

Pastoral activity is understood as an apostolic endeavor. The Council says: "The goal of apostolic endeavor is that all who are made children of God by faith and baptism should come together to praise God in the midst of his Church, to take part in the sacrifice and to eat the Lord's supper" (Constitution on Sacred Liturgy, n. 10). *We may, therefore, conclude that "pastoral" relates to that quality of concern that forms, supports, and aids the human (Christian) expression of life within the community.*

"Pastoral perspectives" must be a quality of all hierarchical structures as well as of any form of lay ministry. "Pastoral" does not stand in opposition to hierarchy, rather it must permeate every dimension of human activity, lay activity as well as hierarchical activity, that attempts to translate God's infinite love into the tangible expressions of human life. Every ministry in the Church must have a "pastoral" quality if it wants to be truly an expression of the Christian community.

In this light I define pastoral ministry as:

> The activation of human abilities, on an individual or organized level, for the sake of the human (Christian) community to foster within this community the growth of the life of the Spirit and the love of God.

This definition focuses on the following points:

1. The development of human abilities for a responsible and professional response to the needs of society.

2. The search for an integration of material and spiritual values in human life.

3. Human participation in the redemptive presence of Christ.

Health care ministry is a special focus on the understanding of ministry, which includes in a particular way, the concern for human wholeness and integration at times of illness. It includes the physical as well as the emotional and spiritual well-being of the patients. Health care ministry focuses on the total person. Because of the inseparable unity of the material, emotional, and spiritual dimensions of human existence, the concern for physical wholeness has a direct bearing on the form in which an individual will respond to other persons and to God. Material qualities of life strongly influence the psychological and spiritual dimensions of each person. Thus ministry, especially health care ministry, is not an addition to or an imposition upon human relationships. It belongs to the human reality. It is a perspective of human life and an expression of religious values. It is therefore a mandate for the Church or for the Christian community.

The Church is a
community of people
who have accepted
the responsibility to
manifest in their
lives and activity
the redemptive love
of God.

CHAPTER TWO

Health Care Ministry:
A Mandate to the Church

In the previous chapter my focus was that human reality by its nature is called to participate in ministry. However, just as the human being does not exist or live or act in isolation but in community with others, so also is a person's involvement in ministry connected with a community. This community is the Church or any religious congregation. In the final analysis it is the congregation that performs ministry through individuals rather than individuals on their own. Although we accept that God (in Christ) is alive and present with every individual believer, it is through the believing community that Christ's redeeming presence is continued on earth.

I see ministry as *an active participation of the community in the redemptive mission of Christ.* In Christ, God assumed human nature to bring redemption to humanity. It was Christ's mission to restore within the human community their original goal of being the living image and created reality of God's life on earth. Jesus started this mission during his earthly life, and after his death and resurrection he continues it in the Church. The Church, however, is not merely an organization; *it is a community of people who have accepted the responsibility to manifest in their lives and activity the creative and redemptive love of God. As such they have inherited from Christ the task to bring salvation to people by reaching out in mutual concern to all who are in need.*

The Church is not a monolithic community. Because the Church is a community of people who believe in Christ, there is a doctrinal unity, but the manner in which this doctrine is lived is greatly influenced by the culture and personality of those who live it. Differences in culture and personality determine largely the manner and internal depth of human concern for others. Differences in organizational structure influence the form in which ministerial activity is expressed.

Jesus' concern for the sick and the needy is very evident in all the gospel accounts. Healing of illnesses of any kind (cf., Mk. 3–4) was a significant part of his ministry. The Acts of the Apostles show that this same concern was passed on to the early Christian communities. These early communities responded to Christ's mandate in different ways, but the same love and dedication was at the center of their response. The same is true today. Different communities respond in different ways to the mandate of ministry. In the following pages I want to reflect on the relationship between Church organization and ministry from three perspectives: The Church as: (1) a community of believers, (2) a structured community, and (3) a source of health care ministry.

THE CHURCH: COMMUNITY OF BELIEVERS

The Church as a community of believers is at the same time a *grace-filled* organization and a *grace-giving* interaction. From both angles the gracing presence of God in Christ lies at the heart of the Church. Organization must be at the service of the gracing presence, which is alive through human interaction.

The Church as Grace-filled Organization

Redemption is not achieved as the sanctification of individuals in isolation but of persons who live and interact within a community. It is the Church's teaching that this community itself is grace-filled.

The New Catholic Encyclopedia says:

> The Church is the sacrament of the triune God's communion with humanity as this is revealed and realized in the two "advocates" of even sinful humanity, "Jesus" (1 Jn. 2:1) and the "other paraclete" the Holy Spirit (Jn. 14:26). The Church is, thus, a double communion—of God with man and of man with God.[2]

The Dogmatic Constitution on the Church states that:[3]

> ...The Church, in Christ, is in the nature of a sacrament—a sign and instrument, that is of communion with God and of unity with all people (n. 1).

The Council further states that the Church is constituted by God:

> The almighty Father created the universe and chose to raise up humankind to his own divine life (n. 2).

> When humanity had fallen in Adam, he did not abandon them, but at all times held out to them the means of salvation (n. 2).

> The Son, accordingly, came, sent by the Father who, before the foundation of the world chose us and predestined us in him for adoptive sonship (n. 3).

> To carry out the will of the Father, Christ inaugurated the kingdom of heaven on earth and revealed to us his mystery; by his obedience he brought about our redemption (n. 3).

> The Church, this is the kingdom of Christ—
> already present in mystery, grows visibly
> through the power of God in the world (n. 3).

Upon his return to the Father, Jesus sent the Holy Spirit, the Paraclete, as he had promised in order that he might continue to sanctify the Church.

> Hence the universal Church is seen to be "a
> people brought into unity from the unity of
> the Father, the Son and the Holy Spirit" (n. 4).

The nature of the Church is made known in images such as:

> The kingdom / reign of God: Mt. 1:15; 4:12.

> Seed sown in the field: Mt. 4:14, waiting to
> sprout: Mt. 4:26–29.

> Images of the sheepfold: Jn. 10:1–10;
> A cultivated field: 1 Cor. 3:9.
> A building of God: 1 Cor. 3:9; Mt. 21:42.

The imagery found in numbers 5 and 6 of *Lumen gentium* confirms both the invisible character of the Church and its visibility.[4] The Church must reach beyond its visible structure. The visible assembly, insofar as it is visible, does not constitute the Church. The assembly must be filled with the presence of God and must manifest this presence in concrete living. Because God is by his nature invisible and beyond human observation, his presence must be made visible in signs through which the spiritual presence and value is expressed in human fellowship. Christopher Butler, in his book *Theology of Vatican Council II,* says it in this way:

> Sacraments, therefore, presume a fellowship
> of men living on earth who have to commu-

nicate by physical signs. If the Church has sacraments at its core and as the source and sustenance of its life, the Church is a concrete human fellowship. As fellowship tending to community, it needs a structure; only through social structure a number of human individuals become a community. There is thus no incoherence between the Council's vision of the Church as basically sacramental and its presentation of the same Church, on earth, as a visible structured human community.[5]

Fellowship needs community and community needs structure. The visibility is brought about in signs—the external manifestation and the reality of the mystery of Christ's presence—and thus the Church is a sign that is grace-filled (because of *divine* presence) and grace-giving (because of God's *redemptive* presence). The Church is sacramental. The understanding of the Church as mystery is essential for the understanding of ministry.

The Church as Grace-giving Human Interaction— People of God

The expression of God's life in the concrete reality of the human assembly constitutes the People of God. God's life is not individualistic or isolated. God's life is triune. This means that its fullness is constituted by a constructive, life-giving reaching out between Father, Word, and Spirit. Therefore, the People of God cannot come about merely by the dedication of individual persons to God and to his service. *To be the People of God demands an active participation in bringing this life of God to a perceptible expression in human life and relationships.* Christ restored to humanity the ability to live this life. The community of believers, characterized by a constructive and mutual reaching out, is the living manifestation of the Christ-life in human reality. This life is the heart of the community. Authority and external structures are essential for the Church's visibility in this world, but they will be empty and meaningless if the deeper meaning of the People of God is not lived in the human setting.

"To be at the service of" does not mean "to be at the command of." Service is something that comes about when people develop fellowship. It is primarily a relationship of freedom in which assistance is rendered for the benefit of others without losing one's own dignity and wholeness. Service is a mutually enabling involvement of all members for the happiness, security, and growth of all. The form in which service is expressed flows forth from the people themselves in response to the origin and nature of the assembly. A destructive activity can never be a service. People—even by majority vote—cannot develop a form of service that would contradict the nature of the assembly and its purpose without destroying the assembly itself.

The task of the assembly, the People of God or the Church, is the salvation of all. Salvation, too, is not an individual matter. The human person is by nature a social being in need of others and in need of relationship, as Butler says:

> While every genuinely conscientious person
> will be saved, salvation itself is not a private
> possession but a participation in a common,
> communal, social salvation.[6]

This participation in a common, communal, social salvation is a participation or sharing in the mission of Christ. Men and women are Christian to the extent that they give themselves in faith and love to Christ and to each other. Through the living sacrifice of their lives, they become the sacrament of Christ's own sacrificial offering to all people[7] and they share in the priestly, prophetic, and kingly mission of Jesus.

Christian life is *priestly* because it is the fulfillment of Christ's mission and places before God all human strivings and activities. It shares in Christ's priestly nature. Priesthood in its most universal sense is the life and the lifestyle that offers to the Father the spiritual values and mission given by God to the community. It gives honor and worship to God through life and prayer. Priesthood is a participation in the sacramental expression (grace-filled sign) of Christ's presence. Christian life demands active participation in the life-giving presence of Christ and not merely passive acceptance of it.

Christian life is also *prophetic*. A prophet is a mediator of God's word of salvation. He or she is the spokesperson for God either in word or in action or both. Christian life itself must speak of God. "Your light must shine before people so that they can see the good things you do and give praise to your Father in heaven" (Mt. 5:16).

Christian life is *kingly* because it establishes a community in which God's life is lived. The community provides the organization needed for the visibility of the redemptive presence of Christ; at the same time it conveys a dignity because of its sharing in the life of Christ. In this community (assembly), the Spirit works and guides infallibly through ordinary and extraordinary gifts. These gifts are given by God for the good of the community. They are the charisma that unite the community and guide it forward toward fullness in Christ. Authority is the organ to maintain and promote the unity and tradition of faith in all. Thus in the People of God there are two major dimensions (it would be inaccurate to call them categories or divisions because that would contradict its deepest meaning), which cannot exist fully without each other:

Hierarchy — *Hierarchy gives a human face to the structure* that makes fellowship possible; it gives visibility to the assembly and is the external bond that brings unity and allows the formation of a community.

— *It constitutes the structure* in which the teaching of Jesus is kept alive, and in which the Spirit and his working can be discerned, although the working of the Spirit does not depend on the structure and is not confined to the structure.

— *It offers a framework for sanctification* because the celebration of the sacramental presence of Christ takes place within the community and thus brings the grace-giving presence of Christ within human reach.

Laity — *Laity are all those who are incorporated into the universal priesthood through Baptism,* who are not ordained but are called to active worship. They form together with the hierarchy the living body made visible through structures.
— *They give witness through sanctity of life* and they participate in creation and redemption by living in the material world and by incorporating Christ's message into the secular social surroundings.
— *They bring Christ's love and presence to others* by ministering in prophetic witness and charity in the service of human growth and in response to human needs.

It is through the total interwovenness of hierarchy and laity that the People of God is alive and visible and that the mission of Christ is carried out.

The Church as a Community Called to Holiness

The Church as a community of believers extends by its nature a call to holiness to all its members. Holiness is the personal surrender of an individual to God. The life of Christ is the most perfect surrender of a human being to God, the most perfect response of the human family to the Creator, and thus established the most complete unity between God and humanity. Christ's life on earth was the initiation of God's visible, sanctifying presence with humanity. After Christ's death and resurrection, this unity and sanctifying presence with humanity is continued in the assembly of believers. Life in the community and of the community must be the visible reality of this sanctifying presence. Christ's body is holy, and consequently, the assembly that expresses his life must be holy too. This call to holiness and its corresponding responsibility is certainly directed to each individual, but beyond the individual it is directed as well to the assembly as a whole. No individual can live and be sanctified in total isolation. Everyone needs forms of interaction with other people that are constructive and sanctifying. Therefore, the call to holiness rests on the assembly as on a community of sanctifying interaction between believers.

Holiness includes giving witness to God's call and enduring the adversities of life that are connected with this witnessing. The call to holiness comes to us first in Baptism through which we enter into the community of God's people and are made sharers in the life of Christ. Of those who are baptized, Vatican Council II says: "...they must hold on to and perfect in their lives that sanctification which they have received from God" (LG 40).

This witness can be given in many different ways and forms. It can be given by laity in their daily interaction with the material world. It can be given in the state of single life or of marriage. Religious life is a branch and a special expression of this call to holiness, but it does not essentially differ from the call of the Christian community. Religious life represents in human terms a total dedication of the individual to God, but it is as a member of the community. Because of the totality of its dedication to God's service, religious life has an eschatological meaning and is a message to the community. It is eschatological in that its total dedication expresses that the ultimate fulfillment of mankind can only be achieved in union with God. As a message it calls the Christian community to the integration of God's values in human existence.

The Church Called to Manifest God's Presence in the World

Vatican Council II emphasized the concept "People of God" to describe the Church. It does not merely refer to a structure or an organization. It refers to a community whose life and goals are centered around Christ as the manifestation of God's presence with humanity. In this light the community of the Church is a call to all humanity to recognize its own dignity and to discover the full meaning of its existence. This discovery and self-knowledge would be impossible without an understanding of the living Christ.

Vatican Council II states:

> It is only in the mystery of the Word made
> flesh that the mystery of human existence
> truly becomes clear (GS 22).

When Christ, the Word Incarnate, revealed his love and union with the Father, he also revealed the full dignity of human existence. Christ revealed in his own life and interhuman relationship what humanity is called to be and how it is called to share in the life of God. Earlier we have seen that living in society is an essential requirement to share in the life of the triune God. Therefore, the Council says:

> Life in society is not something accessory to
> man himself: through his dealings with oth-
> ers, and through fraternal dialogue, man
> develops all his talents and becomes able to
> rise to his destiny (GS 25).

Contemporary technological development, which seems to make people more independent, also increases human interdependence. Human beings must work for the common good:

> which is the sum total of social conditions
> which allow people, either as groups or as
> individuals, to reach their fulfillment more
> fully and more easily (GS 26).

Society must search for a balance. In times of progress there is always a danger that individuals will be sacrificed to the good of the community, particularly to material development in society. This is contrary to the teaching of Jesus. The Church must stand up against it (cf., GS 26). On the other hand, the individual cannot stay aloof from the community because social obligations "must be considered as belonging to man's chief duties" (GS 30).

Active human involvement in the development of the world is the unfolding and fulfillment of God's mysterious design (GS 34); it transforms man and society and gives fulfillment to the individual as well (GS 35).

Earthly affairs have their own autonomy:

> By the very nature of creation, material being is endowed with its own stability, truth and excellence, its own order and laws (GS 36).

Material beings are not an end in themselves. They are part of the total creation that is called to reveal the greatness of God. They are to be used in the perspective of God's self-revelation and not exclusively for the satisfaction of the human person (GS 35). They share in the manifestation of God's presence in material visibility.

Although one must heed the warning of Christ in Lk. 9:25—that to gain the whole world has no profit if one loses oneself (spiritually)—the fulfillment of one's earthly duties and one's contributions to the progress of material creation are a participation in the pascal mystery, which is vital for the kingdom of God (GS 39).

This is a task that the assembly of people (the Church) fulfills mostly through the laity who are called to bear witness to God's presence in the world through their daily life (AA 2). They are called to be the leaven of the community.

The Role of the Church

With the foregoing as our foundation we may describe the Church in the broadest sense as:

> *A community of people united for the communication, manifestation, and preservation of Christ's life on earth. One enters into this community through Baptism. This community is maintained and preserved through interhuman exchange*

> *rooted in a faith that is lived out in unfailing and*
> *unselfish giving for others.*

In view of this, the following characteristics belong to the role of the Church:

1. *Church and world interpenetrate.* The Church, being both a visible society and a spiritual communion, gives divine life to people who live in the world. She assists them to live their life in the world more effectively, particularly through the sacraments and acts of interhuman concern.

2. *The Church gives to individuals a deeper sense of personal dignity,* a sense of freedom, and a call for self-realization by reaching out to others.

3. *The Church offers to society a commitment to foster unity.* She gives meaning to cultural expressions and development; she teaches and keeps alive a concern for all who are in need.

4. *The Church proposes to human activity an integrative being.* She takes away the dichotomy between professionalism in daily life and the profession of faith.

5. *The Church receives from society the language in which to speak the message of God* and integrates the culture so that this message can be lived and manifested.

Thus the Church as community of believers is indeed a source and center of ministry. It is a community that nurtures mutual interaction leading to growth, wholeness, and holiness.

THE CHURCH: A STRUCTURED COMMUNITY

The Church is a community and, therefore, it includes interhuman relationships and organizational structure. Both elements are essential. They interact and, to a certain extent, shape each other. Believers will experience the Church primarily as community or as organization according to where the emphasis is placed. The difference of focus is closely related to the attitudes of the leadership. The way the Church is experienced, in turn, greatly influences the manner by which the call to leadership and ministry will be understood.

Avery Dulles presented five "models of the Church" as ways the Church can be understood and experienced, according to differences in emphasis.[8] None of these models occur in its pure form at any place or time; some elements will always intermingle in each model. However, one thrust will usually surface as the predominant tendency within the universal or local Church at certain periods in history, strongly influencing the manner in which ministry will be performed.

The Church as Institution

When the Church is primarily seen as *institution,* the emphasis will fall on authority and organization. There is a solid scriptural basis for this emphasis. "All authority has been given to me. Go therefore and make disciples of all nations, baptizing them in the name of the Father and of the Son and of the Holy Spirit, teaching them to observe all that I have commanded you" (Mt. 28:18–20). In the focus on the Church as institution the authority (or leadership) is likely to assume all responsibility for the proper execution of the "prophetic," the "sanctifying," and the "ruling" roles that Christ entrusted to it. In this model, the priest is the representative of the authority and assumes responsibility for the teaching, sanctifying, and organizational elements on the local level. Others (laity) can be allowed to participate, but they have little personal responsibility.

Obviously, this model will bring order and clarity. Teaching authority and leadership functions will be sharply delineated, and they will be executed by the hierarchy and its representatives. Doctrine is carefully formulated and presented. Very little is left to individual initiative and responsibility. Spontaneous activity and involvement of the community at large are limited. When all responsibility is placed in the hands of the hierarchy, opportunities for personal growth through involvement are restricted. Many needs will not be effectively responded to, and the Church will be perceived as a clerical institution.

This has also the danger that scientific development is not sufficiently encouraged. Information remains one-sided and open discussion will be difficult. Perhaps the clearest example of this is the recent Apostolic Letter Motu Proprio of Pope John Paul II, *Ad tuendom fidem,* of May 28, 1998, adding a new paragraph to canon 750 of the Code of Canon Law: "Each and everything set forth definitively by the magisterium of the Church regarding teaching on faith and morals must be firmly accepted and held." This approach does not encourage responsible lay participation.

The Church as Communion

When the Church is primarily seen as a communion, the focus shifts from authority and organization to constructive and creative interaction between the members. Authority is not rejected, but its role is different. The emphasis lies here upon co-responsibility. In this approach the Church becomes the People of God, who together carry the responsibility for the message of Christ. All possess and are possessed by the same Spirit who calls and inspires the members to a variety of tasks.

This community-responsibility is more than a "canonical mission" given by authority and accepted by the laity. It is the formation of one body whose members strive for the fulfillment of the message of the gospel. This form does not oppose authority, but rather gives it a new meaning. Authority is not a power hovering over and above the community. It is rather the responsible center in the search for truth. In this model the authority's question is not primarily: "Are the rules of the Church observed?" but "Where does the Spirit of God move the community?" or "How can we recognize in a certain movement the Spirit of God?" On the part of the people the first question is not: "What does a certain authority tell us to do?" but "How can the love of God be best lived in today's society?"

The answer to both questions may coincide, but the leadership will make fewer "authority decisions" (independent from the community); decisions will come forth from both the community and leadership through a joint, communal search for truth. In this way all can stand behind the decision and assume responsibility for it. There is a collaboration and oneness between authority and members.

One of the major advantages of this model is that the community as a whole begins to assume responsibility. All are involved in the process of growth toward personal maturity in faith and charity. This model also has disadvantages. One of them is the danger of developing a form of horizontalism (the voice or opinion of everyone has equal value) that destroys leadership. There is also the possibility of the opposite: that individuals will hold on too rigorously to their own opinion, resulting in danger for division and chaos.

The Church as Sacrament

The Dogmatic Constitution on the Church uses the word "Sacrament" to indicate the deeper meaning of the Church (LG 1). There is a special strength in considering the Church as sacrament. It is then seen as the in-mystery-manifestation of Christ, the visible sign in which Christ expresses the reality of his presence among us. The Church is the continuation of Christ in a much more real sense than any other human institution can ever be the continuation of the work of its founder. The strength and meaning of this model lies in the stress on the living and real presence of Christ. Christ is understood as being simultaneously the authority of the Father and the relationship of love that unites humanity with each other and with God.

This form helps to integrate authority and community into a wholeness of being. Its focus lies on the sanctifying interaction of all members, regardless of their function. It does not allow for a static understanding of the Church but asks for a continual search for deepening and growth.

In the "Church as Sacrament," the community of believers shares in the life of Christ as a "royal priesthood" and as a "people set apart." This perspective is especially important for ministry. If the Church is the representation (or the reality) of Christ's presence, then every member shares in this representation, and each individual member is called to participate in the growth of this Christ-life. To be a member of the body of Christ is a compelling call for compassion, particularly because the suffering of Christ holds such a central place in the mystery of redemption.

There is a danger for the development of narcissism or individualistic elitism because of this deep and personal sharing in the life of Christ. To counteract this there is a need to develop a spirituality that "sharing the life of Christ" means "serving all." There is also the serious danger that if sacramental life becomes too ritualized, it may become shallow and legalistic.

The Church as Herald

The core of this Church model is emphasis on the firm obligation to proclaim the gospel, but it says little about the responsibility for the Church living "as community." This is largely left to individual efforts. The model projects a kind of sacred indifference toward human needs and, on the part of authority, a certain special recognition is granted for task performance. The role of the community with regard to struggle and suffering is limited.

It is clear that without proclamation, God's Word and the mystery of his presence cannot be communicated. The Word of God itself is sacramental. However, the emphasis on proclamation can create a protective shield that prevents true community living and that does not take sufficiently into account the woundedness of the community.

The Church as Servant

In the first four models the Church considers the world the recipient of its activities: (1) The Church teaches, sanctifies, and rules; (2) The Church as God's people grows toward perfection; (3) The Church is the visible manifestation of God's grace; (4) The Church is the proclaimer of the divine message. However, the Church's task is not only to offer its riches to the world, but, because it exists and lives in the world, it also must learn from the world. The Church must be one with the world's joys and sufferings. Through suffering the Church comes face to face with its own imperfections and is called to share in the process of sanctification of every dimension of human existence. From the world the Church learns the language and receives the culture in which the message of the gospel is to be proclaimed and which, in turn, must be sanctified through this message.

These five models are deeply intertwined in the reality of daily life. Although at different times and in different circumstances certain forms may receive more emphasis, at no point can a single approach be found in its pure form.

Each form has its own importance for health care ministry. Ministry must be filled with a spirit of compassion and love. It must present the reality of Christ's presence among us, but it also needs structure, proclamation, and service. Contemporary and local needs will adapt and modify the approaches to this ministry.

THE CHURCH:
SOURCE OF HEALTH CARE MINISTRY

Health care ministry in its broadest sense means "to be at the service of human wholeness." It means to activate and integrate the physical, emotional, and spiritual values in an individual at a time when an imbalance has occurred in his or her life. The more clearly this call for wholeness is understood, professed, and experienced, the more the service to those who experience imbalance (illness) will be seen as a demand and mission.

The Church is the place where this vision of wholeness must be most intensely understood and lived because the Church is called to be the visible expression of the life of Christ in the community. Whether the Church is presented as the People of God or as a structured community is, in itself, not of essential importance. The central point is that health care ministry, or the ministry of human wholeness (physical and spiritual integration), is inseparable from the mission of the Church. Without involvement in healing ministry, the message of Christ would not be fully expressed. The following points illustrate what I mean:

1. The Church is established as the life of Christ with humanity and as the redemptive process of human life in Christ.

2. The nature and depth of the Christ-life is made visible in this world through physical-psychological reality.

3. The spiritual nature and the physical-psychological human reality are deeply interwoven and mutually interact so as to create a personal balance for each individual.

4. The more these spiritual and physical-psychological dimensions can be integrated, the healthier (the more wholesome) a person *as person* will be.

5. The imbalance caused by physical (or emotional) illness can endanger the total health of an individual person.

6. The new personal value dimension (and balance) created by illness asks for a special expression of concern in the psychological as well as in the spiritual aspects of individual life.

7. The Church as the visible realization of God's creative and redemptive love has a special task in the concern for the sick.

The content and meaning of the ministry of healing in the mission of Christ is a subject for later reflections. First I want to focus on the object of health care ministry: human suffering.

As far as can
be observed, pain
and suffering are
so intimately
connected with
human existence
that one must accept
that they belong to
"being human."

CHAPTER THREE

Pain and Suffering:
A Human Reality

No one in his or her right mind seeks suffering for suffering's sake, yet, no one alive in this world can remain without suffering for a long time. Throughout the thousands of years of human history humanity has searched for ways to avoid pain and suffering, or rather humanity searched for ways to overcome it and to bring it under control of human powers. Despite enormous progress in science and technology, humanity is still as far away from a solution as ever before in history. When a solution has been found for one problem another pops up at another place. As far as can be observed at this time in history, pain and suffering are so intimately and inseparably connected with human existence that one must accept that they belong to "being human."

The words "pain" and "suffering" are often used together and sometimes interchanged. However, there is a difference. *Pain* refers to the conscious experience of (physical, emotional, or spiritual) discomfort usually beyond the control of the individual, which may (or may not) hinder the normal self-expression of the person. *Suffering* on the other hand, goes beyond the conscious experience of discomfort. It includes a certain *knowledge* of the influence of pain upon one's life and an *attitude* of acceptance, indifference, or rejection with regard to the pain/discomfort.

I mentioned that the conscious experience of pain and/or

suffering can be physical, emotional, or spiritual. This depends on the originating source. Because these three aspects of human life are inseparably intertwined and interactive in human existence, when one is affected by a discomfort, there are repercussions also on the other two aspects. A serious headache is more than merely physical. It will in some way affect one's relationship with others and one's relationship with God. A strong emotional experience will influence one's physical effectiveness, and the relationship with God will have its impact upon the peace of mind and physical abilities of an individual. The relationship between the physical, emotional, and spiritual dimensions in human life is different for every individual. They come to a certain balance in which each one finds a way of existing that is most comfortable for him/her at this moment of existence. This balance changes constantly and tries to adapt to the demands and circumstances of life. Even in pain and suffering the individual tries to find a way to make life as livable as possible. This search for balance is typically expressed in questions such as *"Why?," "Why me?," "How can I handle this situation?," "What is happening to me?"* and many others. These questions represent the conscious or unconscious search for understanding, a new balance, or a readjustment that will make life once again livable.

Although pain and suffering touch the total human reality of body, mind, and spirit, they are experienced primarily in the physical reality of life because we exist and have our identity in the physical world. Our discussion, therefore, centers on the physical reality but includes emotional and spiritual aspects as well. These are our primary topics:

1. The role of the body in human life.

2. Health and illness influence and shape human responsibility.

3. The human experience of pain and suffering.

4. The process of loss and grieving.

5. Illness in interhuman perspective.

THE ROLE OF THE BODY IN HUMAN LIFE

The human body is more than a biochemical composition. It is a physical reality animated (ensouled) by the human spirit yet, despite its emotional qualities and "spiritual" connection, it remains subject to all characteristics and limitations of material existence. It is, therefore, more accurate to describe the body as *"the human person seen from the perspective of and presence in time and space."* Four major aspects describe the role and function of the body in human life.

The Body Defines Our Presence in This World

Our body gives us an awareness of where we are. It places us in a physical relationship to our surroundings. Because of our body, we know that we are in a specific location, in the company of specific people. We experience health and sickness, strength and weakness, fatigue and energy, in our body. Our relationship with others is normally established through bodily presence. Closeness and remoteness are bodily as well as psychological experiences. Even the ability to relate to others, to think of them and to love them, needs bodily qualities. Talents and skills, too, have a bodily basis without which they cannot operate. The body indicates the limitations of our physical human potential, even though it develops an ease to perform many of our activities such as speaking and walking. Briefly, without the body we cannot be in this world and relate to each other. Bodily experience lies at the center of human identity.

The Body Influences Our Self-image

Cosmetics is big business. Our appearance is an important factor in how we feel about ourselves. We recognize ourselves in the face we see in the mirror. A scar on the face is much more likely to cause self-consciousness than one that remains after an appendectomy. The importance of physical appearance and wholeness is still more evident when a person has suffered the loss of a limb. I remember the instance of the gentleman, a capable engineer of heavy road equipment, who had lost an arm in an accident. Even after perfect healing and successful rehabilitation and job-retraining, he remained bitter and made life miserable for his wife and daughter. In counseling, it soon became evident that he saw himself not as a whole person but as a handicapped, one-armed engineer. It was only when he began to see himself as an exceptionally capable one-armed engineer, that he could find peace in his own mind and make life pleasant for his family. The loss of his arm meant for him the loss of self-confidence and self-respect. This man had to learn to accept himself as he was after the accident. Our basic self-image is usually closely related to our body image. This becomes acutely important when we remember that we need our body to relate to others. When there is a substantial change in our bodily appearance, we feel as if we are a different person and this involves (at least in our mind) a change in our relationship with other people.

The Body Co-determines Our Contribution to Society

Any interhuman relationship demands some form of perceptible expression. It is only through the body that this can be done. Our bodily activity also suggests the degree to which we are involved in society. For example, it is one thing to be deeply concerned about poverty in certain areas of the world; it is another to be actively involved in the alleviation of hunger. An intellectual (and even an emotional) concern suggests a different form (and often degree) of involvement than being actively engaged in agriculture, transportation, or other ways to address human concerns.

This bodily engagement is not the ultimate norm to evaluate participation in the alleviation of human needs, but it does play an important role in determining the meaning of involvement. Similarly, when we consciously hurt other people, the degree of physical violence suggests the degree of anger within us. Absence of involvement may reveal the degree of lack of concern for others. The contribution that society expects of a healthy person is different from the contribution that is expected from the handicapped. Each one must act according to one's personal abilities, but these abilities are co-determined by the body.

The Body Shares in Our Relationship with God

God created humanity as part of this material world even though human life transcends material existence. The response or service that God expects from humanity must, therefore, be manifested and performed in material dimensions. The body is not merely an instrument that we use in order to carry out God's will. It is the ambience, the co-determining element that constitutes the human presence in this world. It is the external form of human activity and of human service to God. Without bodily involvement our activity is not fully human.

Thinking about love is not the same as loving. Loving in our minds is not as effective and total as expressing love in our lives and activities. Through mutual concern people contribute to each other's growth as persons. Every individual is called to be co-creator with God. People collaborate with God through the development of their own talents and through constructive support that each one can give for the growth of others. All people are called to be co-redeemers with Christ. People collaborate with Christ through reaching out lovingly to others and responding to them. In our human condition these forms of participation in creation and redemption are impossible without the body. The human heart and mind are indispensable requirements for a personal relationship with God.

These four aspects of the role of the body touch the heart of human self-realization. When the body is affected by illness, the total person is in a certain degree of disarray. In such cases, steps need to be taken either to restore the previous balance or to find a new balance to make life acceptable. There is no physical disease that is merely physical. Nor is there an emotional illness that is merely emotional. Any form of illness always affects the person in his or her totality.

HEALTH AND ILLNESS INFLUENCE AND SHAPE HUMAN RESPONSIBILITY

It is a rather common human attitude to consider health and perfection as blessings while illness is understood as a curse unworthy of human existence. The progress of medical science and technology makes it very difficult for the present generation to accept illness and suffering as basic human realities and to understand the ability to suffer as a fundamental prerequisite for the appreciation of health.

The human being is created in the image of God. *The deepest meaning of "image," however, does not lie in any form or degree of physical perfection but rather in responsible self-determination within the limitations of one's actual existence.* The condition in which one is at a certain moment is the concrete reality and basis for the authentic human response to God and to one's fellow human beings. Antonellus Elsasser,[9] in his article *Gesundheit und Krankheit,* explains in seven consecutive steps what this responsibility means in human life and what the ethical perspectives of this responsibility are.

Health and Illness are Inseparable from the Human Experience

Human life is a continual process of unfolding, organizing, reorganizing, and integrating. We see this in physical life when cell-divisions build organisms and organ-systems that constitute the individual. This is also true for emotional / psychological life in which intelligence and emotions develop and grow through interaction with other persons and nature. This same process applies to spiritual life as we learn to respond to God in a personal way.

The important factor is that a human being is always "in

process" toward the realization of a perfect equilibrium. Physical existence is constantly subject to change. Psychological and emotional growth demands that a person leave the familiar conditions of life behind and enter into the unknown. Every individual searches for a general structure of life in which he or she finds the highest degree of comfort one can produce at this time. An affirmative and appropriate response to this structure leads to a certain degree of harmony (or health) and internal rest, while a negative response leads to disharmony and internal unrest. Due to human limitations, harmony is not always achieved, and disharmony cannot always be avoided. At the heart of all human growth is the quest for balance. On this journey successes and failures are alternating necessities. Thus health and illness are both experiences without which human life cannot exist.

Health and Illness Affect the Total Person

Health and illness are not simply realities that can be dealt with on a purely material or biochemical level. Nor are they isolated realities that exist totally independent from one another. Vatican Council II is clearly concerned about a holistic approach to human life, and Jesus was never solely concerned with physical healing. His concern was with the whole person.

Illness does not merely affect the human organism. It is an imbalance in the person. A person experiences an illness as an alienation from what one feels called to be and as a limitation of his or her power of personal self-realization. We express this in the popular saying "I am not myself." The body is the place where the physical and spiritual dimensions of human life intertwine and integrate. When physical illness impedes the expected functioning of the body, when the usual or conscious integration of human functions does not take place, then the experience of that moment seems alien to the person whom we know that we are. From this viewpoint it is correct to say that physical illness causes a breach between the "self" and the body. The sick person is not him or her self. There is a "personal" imbalance which causes a disharmony in the customary relationships with self and others. Health and illness do not only affect the body, they truly affect the total person.

Health and Illness Influence the Fulfillment of Personal and Social Life

Because the person, not merely the organism, is the subject of health and illness, the individual's physical and emotional condition is a co-determining factor in the person's response to life. The human response to life remains a personal mandate. Each person must assume responsibility for his or her life the way it is. This is not to say that people are always responsible for being ill, but that they remain responsible for their life, behavior, and growth also during illness. This theory seems to be contrary to the contemporary tendency to reduce illness wholly to an organic defect. Even if it is not stated in these exact terms, it is confirmed by a rather general attitude that an illness can be cured by purely physical means. We can see this attitude in the tendency to keep organic functions alive even when all "human" functions have ceased. If this attitude reflected the truth, then health would simply become a biochemical condition, and there would be little *personal* responsibility for one's health. Human experience contradicts this materialistic theory. Personal attitudes have a great influence upon the health of an individual. Furthermore, the gospels show that Jesus was concerned with the total person: "You are cured now, but don't sin anymore" (Jn. 5:11). St. Paul seems to reflect the same opinion when he warns that disregard for the laws of God brings judgment, and he adds: "That is why many of you are sick and weak, and several have died" (1 Cor. 11:30). St. James said that: "Prayer made in faith will heal the sick person..." (Js. 5:15). If there is an interaction between the material, emotional, and spiritual dimensions of human existence, then there is also a degree of human responsibility for the maintenance and restoration of one's physical health as part of personal wholeness. Personal responsibilities extend as well to the society in which one lives, because the interaction with society is part of human growth and development. Thus health and illness influence the fulfillment of one's individual and social responsibilities.

Illness and Suffering Remain Inexplicable Human Phenomena

Although responsible behavior contributes to the maintenance of one's health, frequently illness is unavoidable and cannot be blamed on irresponsible behavior. Illness is a human reality that is often inexplicable. Efforts to give theological explanations, such as, "God allows us to suffer for our own good and for our sanctification," are insufficient. Theology has no answer.

When Paul says, "For sin pays its wage ... death" (Rom. 6:23), it may sound as if he considers sinfulness as a cause of illness. In reality, he speaks about the kind of death that is overcome by grace, and about suffering that finds its healing through a new creation. He does not speak about sin as the cause of physical illness.

Jesus himself refused to see suffering as punishment when he said of the man born blind: "Neither he nor his parents sinned; it is so that the works of God might be made visible through him" (Jn. 9:3). They provide an opportunity to manifest the works of God. From human perspective, illness remains a mystery that cannot be explained.

Illness and Suffering Are Limitations that Must Be Dealt with in Human and Christian Ways

For humankind in general and physicians in particular, it is important to remember that illness in and of itself has no purpose. It is the human task to overcome illness. Christ himself reacted against illness. He did not attach any religious meaning to suffering for its own sake. It is therefore quite appropriate that human beings fight it also. However, humanity will never succeed in eliminating all suffering. It is a constitutive element of human existence. Humanity cannot escape suffering. It must integrate suffering into its way of life.

Coping with suffering and illness is neither a sign of passivity or fatalism, nor does it mean a rejection of suffering and illness as unworthy of human life. Coping must be understood from three major perspectives: (1) Illness is not seen as merely an organic defect, but as a reality that touches the center of human life and that may ask for new adaptations to life; (2) Healing is more than physical recovery, it must bring about a change in life as Jesus said, "Look, now you are well. Quit your sins, or something worse may happen to you" (Jn. 5:15); (3) When an illness cannot be cured, coping includes a readiness to learn to live with it as effectively as possible. Illness becomes a constitutive element in the condition of the individual. It will lose its harmful and paralyzing power when life is made productive in new ways. Illness can become an opportunity for discovering unknown talents and for significant human development.

Health and Illness Often Contribute to Interhuman Solidarity

Although illness often seems meaningless, it is an experience of human limitation and, consequently, it can lead to reflection on and arrival at a deeper sense of God's presence with us. Humanity as a whole and every individual within it is called to express God's life and love in human life and relationship. The development and activation of human abilities happens through reaching out to others in an effort for mutual support and deepening of the human relationship with God. In illness, one experiences one's own dependence and brokenness, and thus one's very being cries out for support, understanding, and concern.

Jesus came to heal the sick not primarily by making them aware that they needed a physician but by letting them experience the love (and preference) of God for those who are most in need of help (cf., Mt. 25:36). Illness is a call to acknowledge one's dependence on God as well as a call for interhuman concern. St. John asks: "How can you love God whom you do not see if you don't love your neighbor who is always with you?" (1 Jn. 4:19 ff). Conversely we may ask: "How can anyone know that God loves him or her if one does not (in some form) experience this love from fellow human beings?" The weakened condition of an individual expresses simultaneously a dependence on a power beyond one's control and a request for a supportive response from others. Thus human solidarity deepens, and God's presence is manifested in a special way.

Health and Illness Ask for Personal Communication between Physician and Patient

At several places I have indicated that concern for one's health is the responsibility of each individual. When illness strikes and we must give ourselves into the care of a physician, we do not abdicate our responsibility. Rather, physician and patient must carry this together and become one principle of operation. Honesty and open communication between them are extremely important.

Openness on the part of the patient and concern on the part of the physician are not limited to the physical condition but touch on the total person, including religious dimensions. This does not make the physician a pastor, but this concern for wholeness opens the way for the physician to treat the patient as a whole person and allows for a team effort between pastor and physician.

THE HUMAN EXPERIENCE OF PAIN AND SUFFERING

Nobody wants pain, but at certain points in life everyone experiences it in various forms and degrees of intensity. Many different reasons may be indicated as the cause or source of pain. It may be natural disaster, human negligence or malice, or personal weakness, but in all instances, it is the result of a disorder in the structure of human life, whether it be biological, psychological/emotional, or spiritual. The two major sources that are important for our discussion here are the biological and psychological.

Physical Pain

Physical pain occurs when bodily cells or organisms are threatened or experience harm, and via neurons that threat or harm is forwarded to the brain.[10] The brain decodes the message and it then becomes a conscious experience. Pain is experienced differently by every individual, and the apparent intensity of it depends on many circumstances. As stated in a Mayo Clinic Health Letter: "Pain is unique. The varieties of miseries are as many as its sufferers. Your pain is an interplay of your own particular biological, psychological and cultural makeup."[11] Four simultaneous events converge to influence (and define) the personal experience of physical pain:

1. *The urgency of the message that the neurons send to the brain.* The urgency indicates the intensity/magnitude of the pain experienced by the individual.

2. *The amount and nature of competing activity of other nerves.* Thus it is possible that a certain pain is not felt because other kinds of intense involvement occupy the nerve-system. The fact that pain sometimes disappears from consciousness does not mean that the physical and emotional disorder was or is imaginary. It only indicates that some other involvement or preoccupation prevented the message from getting through to consciousness. The pain will get through, however, as soon as the lines of communication are open again.

3. *The interpretation that the brain gives to the messages.* The uncertainty of the meaning of pain (is it cancer? is it a frac-

ture?) is sometimes more debilitating than the certainty about the nature of a specific pain (kidney stone, gall bladder, heavy bruises).

4. *The ability of the person to handle the interpretation.* To what degree does the capacity to correct the cause of the pain or to integrate it into the fabric of one's life exist? For many (mostly unknown) reasons some persons have a much higher pain tolerance than others.

Physical pain is usually a warning signal that something is wrong and needs attention or care. The continued presence of pain indicates a need for further care; the cessation of pain suggests progress in healing. There is a rare genetic disease that prevents a person from feeling pain. It is known as "Riley Dag Disease Syndrome." (A form of this disease occurs also in leprosy, as related in the biography of Fr. Damian DeVeuster, who discovered that he had leprosy when he scorched his foot in boiling water without experiencing pain.) Consequently, such persons are liable to develop severe wounds that may turn into life-threatening infections without noticing it. In general, pain is a warning signal and plays an important role in human life. We speak here about meaningful pain. This signal may be the first step toward healing.

Some experiences of pain are *meaningless* in as much as they indeed indicate a severe threat to the organism or to life, but there is no prospect for cure or healing. This happens, for instance, in certain forms of cancer. Theodore Bovet, in his article "Human Attitudes Toward Suffering,"[12] points out: "It is an important part of the physician's task to differentiate between pain that must be suppressed in the interest of the patient and pain that should not be masked for the same reason." Meaningless pain serves no purpose and can profitably be suppressed provided that this suppression of pain does not totally eliminate human consciousness if that is possible. The suppression of consciousness affects the exercise of human responsibility. Each case must be evaluated on its own merits. Dorothy

Soelle, in her article, "Suffering and Language,"[13] writes:

> There is pain that renders people blind and
> deaf. Feeling for others dies; suffering iso-
> lates a person and he or she no longer cares
> about anyone but himself . . . Extreme suffer-
> ing turns a person into oneself completely; it
> destroys one's ability to communicate.

Psychological Pain

Psychological pain is the psychic or emotional discomfort
that occurs when a certain dimension of life is threatened or
impeded so that functioning becomes difficult or impossible.
There are as many varieties and degrees of this pain as there
are kinds and degrees of psychological or emotional distur-
bances. I want to focus attention on one of the main sources of
psychological pain.

Depression—Depression is one of the most frequently occur-
ring emotional pains. Robert Goldenson[14] defines it as:

> An emotional state of morbid dejection and
> sadness, ranging from mild discouragement
> and down-heartedness to feelings of utter
> hopelessness and despair.

An in-depth consideration of depression is outside the frame
of these pages, however, I do want to indicate that many forms of
it present themselves frequently in pastoral care contacts.[15] It may
appear in any degree from "feeling down in the dumps" because
of being sick or having a headache to a real depression presenting
some of the diagnostic characteristics[16] such as (1) poor appetite
or overeating, (2) insomnia or hypersomnia, (3) low energy or
fatigue, (4) low self-esteem, (5) poor concentration or difficulty
making decisions, (6) feelings of hopelessness. Serious pathological conditions need to be treated by professionals.

For our purpose it will suffice to discuss the very general division of (a) reactive depression (also called non-endogenous depression) and (b) endogenous depression.

a. *Reactive Depression.* This form occurs when the depression can be traced back to a (clearly) definable cause. It may be caused by physical pain that prevents a person from performing his or her usual activities. It may result from grief over the loss of a loved one, or other possible causes such as: failure in job performance, lack of success in the realization of certain ambitions, unfulfilled hopes, negligence in fulfilling responsibilities with regards to others, and so on.

The immediate effects of such depressions can go in opposite directions, depending on the individual's strength and personality. (1) They can broaden the horizons because they may force a person to consider alternatives. Thus they can lead to new perspectives on life or open one's mind for the needs of others. Or the opposite can happen. (2) They can isolate the individual and lead to egotism, solipsism, or individualism. They can express themselves in self-pity and inactivity. In normal circumstances such reactive depressions wear off when new adjustments have been made through deliberate efforts or because time goes on and forces new ways of life upon the sufferers.

In some instances a reactive depression may activate an underlying (dormant) endogenous depression, for instance, when loved ones were hurt because of real or perceived neglect, a deep personal guilt may begin to control the individual and may call forth a strong inferiority and/or guilt complex. Such cases are often difficult to heal. They have a special kind of pain that touches deeply into the individual's self-respect.

b. *Endogenous Depression.* This kind of depression does not have a recognizable source. It seems to originate from within the individual. Often it is accompanied by an undefinable sadness which has a paralyzing influence. In many instances it may affect the physical condition as well. Frequently there seems to be a connection between an external cause and an endogenous depression, which gives the inaccurate impression that one is dealing with a reactive depression. The endogenous nature of the depression becomes visible when the length and depth of the depression is out of proportion to the external cause from which it seems to originate. For instance, grief over the death of a loved one is good and healthy, but when a person is unable to return to normal life after a great length of time, something else may be going on. When an individual seems unable to handle a depression, we should be alert for a possible pathological condition that may need professional help.

Physical and psychological pain appears in many forms and goes through several phases. Dorothy Soelle, in her book on suffering,[17] proposes the working schema, shown on page 51, to recognize these phases and to suggest possible supportive approaches.

It is the task of pastoral ministry to recognize these phases, to understand their significance for the patient, and to assist the individual to deal appropriately with his or her pain.

Immediate Reactions to Pain and Suffering

Nobody likes to suffer. As soon as danger is sensed, the body reacts automatically in self-protection. The individual tends to withdraw if that is possible, but sometimes pain and suffering are unavoidable. In such cases the more common reactions are:

Sharing one's suffering or pain by talking about it with others. Sharing can be done for a variety of reasons.

    a. Talking about one's experiences with others often brings emotional relief;

Phases in Suffering

PHASE ONE is the first state of shock. What happened is beyond comprehension. The condition may be temporarily paralyzing, even though the individual is not consciously aware of the pain.

PHASE TWO is when the sufferer tries to formulate the situation for him or herself. The individual becomes fully aware of the pain.

PHASE THREE is when the sufferer tries to look at the new situation and makes an effort to integrate the loss and to arrange life accordingly.

PHASE ONE	PHASE TWO	PHASE THREE
mute, numb, explosive	lamenting	changing
speechless	aware, able to speak	organizing
moaning, animal-like wailing	psalmic language, rationality and emotions communicated together	rational language
isolation	expression, communication	solidarity
the pressure of suffering turns one into oneself	the pressure of suffering sensitizes	the pressure of suffering produces solidarity
autonomy of thinking, speaking and acting is lost	autonomy of experience (can be integrated)	autonomy of action that produces change
objectives cannot be organized, reactive behavior	objectives are utopian (in prayer)	objectives can be organized, active behavior
dominated by the situation	suffering from the situation and analyzing it	helping to shape the situation
submissiveness	suffering	
powerlessness	acceptance and conquest in existing structures	acceptance and conquest of powerlessness in changed structures

b. Sharing one's pain with others can be a way of asking for advice. Others may be able to suggest ways to avoid or to diminish suffering;

c. Sharing may be a way to awaken sympathy in others;

d. It may be an effort to control others. An exaggerated concern for sympathy may lead to endless lamentations. In these cases the sharing is more an exploitation of others than a search for healing. A disproportionate need for sympathy may lead to a pathological condition in which an individual nurtures his or her pain in order to get sympathy or other secondary gains.

Using drugs. The use of drugs is perhaps the most common way to escape pain. Excessive pain can seriously impede normal human functioning. To suppress such pain can be most advisable. An excessive use of drugs, however, may indicate an inability to handle reality. Our contemporary approach to life and our present medical practices tend to suppress pain even to the point of completely suppressing the patient's consciousness. This practice has moral implications that need to be considered for each case individually.

Accepting suffering. Acceptance means that active resistance is no longer the center of the patient's attention. This occurs in two significant ways:

a. *Passive resignation.* Passive resignation is a form of total surrender in which all resistance against pain or suffering has stopped. It produces a sort of numbness or fatalistic mentality that considers fighting against pain useless. The sufferer is dominated by a dejected attitude frequently accompanied by bitterness and suppressed anger against all and everything, including God. The pain dominates or controls the life of the individual. Depression is common in such circumstances.

b. *Positive acceptance.* Pain and suffering are incorporated into the individual's behavior and attitude as a dimension of life which, at this time, is unavoidable and which has a role in the fulfillment of one's task at this moment. Dietrich Bonhoefer speaks about "resistance and surrender" in human suffering. He suggests a continued resistance against suffering, yet at the same time he advises a surrender to it. In this context the individual is not controlled by the pain, but he or she remains in charge of his or her life. Suffering becomes then an aspect that is incorporated into the person's approach to achieve self-realization. Positive acceptance is the courage to overcome (or to cope with) suffering and to integrate it into daily life rather than passively submit to it.

Stoicism, recklessness, masochism and many other expressions try to ignore the reality of pain or suffering in the hope that by ignoring it, one does not have to deal with it.

Searching for a deeper meaning in suffering. This reaction is closely related to positive acceptance and will be discussed in the next section.

Efforts to Understand Human Suffering

Three categories of comprehension seem to help us come to a better understanding of human suffering:

1. Some rationale for the cause, reason, and meaning of suffering;

2. Some knowledge of the effects of suffering on human life;

3. A perspective of possible positive effects of suffering.

The **cause and reason of suffering** is usually unknown. Even if one knows exactly how an accident happened or why one is rejected by others, there remains still the question, "Why did it happen at this particular time, to this particular person, and in these particular circumstances?" However, the pain of the accident or rejection remains present and real.

For primitive people there is rarely a purely "natural" cause for accidents or illnesses. These are always the works of God or of spirits. Unfamiliarity with natural causes easily directs the mind to divine intervention; it often increases the sense of powerlessness and may lead to fatalism.

In more sophisticated societies natural (physical) causes are often overemphasized. Frequently one does not search for underlying perspectives or reasons. Life seems to begin and to end with the perceptible. With no other source of support, the loss of one's abilities becomes a source of depression.

Many persons consider suffering as a punishment from God. As a result, in such people there is often a sense of guilt or of incertitude concerning their spiritual condition.

Finally, there are many people who consider suffering to be an aspect of God's plan for personal self-realization and for sanctification of an individual. Many theologians, however, see this approach as contrary to the concept of a loving and merciful God.

Another approach to understanding suffering maintains that there is no answer or explanation. This theory holds that it would be counterproductive to the effort to resist suffering, if suffering had a clear and concrete meaning. However, the attempt to deny any meaning to suffering may easily lead to fatalism and depression.

Suffering for the sake of suffering is meaningless. Only in a human context can suffering find meaning and perspective. This opinion is based upon the actions of Jesus who did not explain why the man who came to him was born blind. Instead, he pointed to the power of God that was revealed in his healing.

The **effects of suffering on human life** are closely related to the way in which suffering is understood and accepted. If suffering is considered to be a punishment, the patient may be plagued with a deep sense of guilt, which in turn stands in the way of healing. If suffering is accepted in a negative manner, as an impediment for self-fulfillment, it may cause a paralyzing fatalism, which makes healing more difficult. If, however, suffering can be accepted positively, as an integral part of one's being at this moment of life, the following effects are more likely to occur:

a. Illness leads to the recognition of a power beyond one's control. In illness one experiences a personal insufficiency, and one becomes explicitly aware of one's dependence on a power that has direct influence on one's life, but which one cannot control. Whether this power is understood as God or as Fate is at this moment irrelevant. The important point is that the individual acknowledges a personal insufficiency.

b. The patient and family must take a personal position with regard to this power. The position may be love or hatred, respect or rejection, fear or peaceful submission, but one cannot ignore this power.

c. One communicates with this power through one's personal response. The content and quality of the response will, obviously, depend on the position that one has taken.

d. Suffering makes the patient aware of his or her limitations. Usually people take health and abilities for granted. Illness disrupts this routine, and one experiences the frailty of human life.

Once one has a certain knowledge of the effects of suffering on human life, it becomes possible to develop a **perspective of what one can do in the present condition.**

a. Hidden talents can be discovered and developed; new resources can be tapped when one's usual activity is impeded. New richness of personality can surface through necessary adjustment to circumstances.

b. Joys and satisfactions on account of new developments frequently overshadow the disappointments caused by the limitations of suffering. The sufferer experiences a new form of inner peace which integrates spiritual and material values.

Suffering teaches us the nature of our true selves. This means it teaches us to display those values and fundamental characteristics which exist independently from external circumstances such as wealth or social position. In order to live authentically we need to know the difference between who we are and what we have.

Meister Eckhart writes:

> Suffering is a fast-footed animal that can carry us in the shortest possible time to the greatest possible perfection.[18]

THE PROCESS OF LOSS AND GRIEVING

The Nature of Loss and Suffering

The experience of pain or of any other form of suffering usually impedes normal daily activity. The degree of the impediment depends on the severity of the pain or on the nature of the sufferer. The normal balance of life is disrupted. The understanding and appreciation of one's human "self" has, at least temporarily, changed.

At the basis of every loss lies an *attachment,* or the condition in which a person has bound him or herself to another person or object. The attachment originates from a combination of reasons. It may be the result of a *need dependency,* either food or reproductive needs, or of a need for *security and safety,* or as in human beings, the need for *development and growth and an affectional bond.*[19] In loss this attachment is broken and the individual experiences an uncomfortable and often painful void. Something that was there is not there anymore. The individual suffers a loss whether temporarily or permanently. In very general terms a loss can be described as: "the experience that an important value, perspective, person, or object has disappeared from one's life so that a reshaping of life and expectations becomes necessary."

Such a loss can occur suddenly, but it can also be the end result of a long process in which, step by step, the individual has witnessed the approaching condition.

For our study the important aspect is not that a change is taking place. I want to focus on *the process by which the individual restores his or her life to its original condition or readjusts him or herself to live effectively in the new situation*. This process is usually an experience of great emotional pain and turmoil. This experience is called the process of grieving.

The Nature of Grieving

There are four critical stages of personal involvement in the complete grieving process:

1. *Accepting the reality of the loss*, or to come face to face with the fact that death/irreversible separation has occurred.

2. *Working through the pain and grief*, allowing the separation to enter into one's affectional life.

3. *Adjusting to an environment in which the deceased is missing.* This includes an adjustment of activities and relationships.

4. *Emotionally relocating the deceased and moving on with life.* The deceased receives a new place in the emotional life of the survivor so that life can continue.[20]

In *The Last Dance. Encountering Death and Dying*[21], Lynne Ann DeSpelder and Albert Strickland say:

Grief is a personal emotional response to an event or loss. Like bereavement, grief has usually been thought of in negative terms: Heartbreak, anguish, distress, suffering—a burdensome, emotional state. Yet, grief can be considered as the TOTAL emotional response to loss. Among the full range of emotions that might be present in the survivor's grief are not only sorrow and sadness, but also relief, anger, disgust, and self-pity. Limiting our definition of grief to any of these emotions reduces the chances of accepting all the emotions that may be present.

Very often grief refers to sadness and sorrow over the loss of a loved one. However, its meaning is also applicable to all other human conditions in which losses occur. The nature and form of grief may differ according to the nature and degree of the loss that is experienced, but the essential elements have usually a great similarity. The various forms and qualities of grief do not always manifest themselves at the same time or to the same degree. When one is dealing with a grieving person, it is necessary to be very sensitive for the individual characteristics of each case. This individual aspect is important because grief is a response to a *personal* loss. It is an *individual* effort to cope or deal with disruptive situations.

Grief, like suffering, cannot be fully understood in the abstract, but only as a concrete human reality. With regard to the individual dimensions of suffering, Gabriel Marcel[21] observed:

I speak of suffering, and I say that suffering is a reality. But yet this is not true. Suffering does not exist abstractly; what exists is YOUR suffering and MINE, THIS suffering and THIS OTHER suffering. When we attempt to gather up all those acts of individual suffering, we instead become very empty-handed. The suffering of nobody in particular is an abstract category, an empty effigy, devoid of real life and specific meaning, serving all purposes and therefore none.

Grief also has its own individual nature. Full pastoral response is only possible if we know the source of the sorrow and the person who is grieving. Frequently we can only see the external characteristics, not the internal source of pain. We must judge by symptoms that may have some validity, but which are never absolutes.

In acute grief there are several symptoms that occur fairly regularly. Erich Lindemann[23] summarizes these as follows:

> …sensations of somatic distress occurring in waves lasting from twenty minutes to an hour at a time, a feeling of tightness in the throat, choking with shortness of breath, need for sighing, and an empty feeling in the abdomen, lack of muscular power, and an intense subjective distress described as tension or mental pain.

These external symptoms are often accompanied by certain emotional conditions:

> There is a loss of warmth and friendliness for others, sometimes even a feeling of hostility toward them. The bereaved wants to be left alone. The bereaved has a strong preoccupation with feelings of guilt, searching for what should have been done to prevent the loss.
>
> The usual conduct changes to a restlessness and inability to concentrate on any task.

It is the task of the minister to see and understand the symptoms in light of the reality of the loss that is suffered and of the person who suffers the loss. Symptoms may indicate special conditions or concerns. When grief lasts much longer, or seems to be much more intense than the nature of the loss would suggest, then there is most likely another (internal?) factor involved and there may be need for professional therapeutic assistance. Sandra Galdieri Wilcox and Marilyn Sutton[24] explain some forms of distorted reactions in the grieving process. These distortions result mostly from alteration in the patient`s feelings and conduct:

1. *Overactivity without a sense of loss.* The individual displays a sense of well-being and zest while his or her activities resemble the activities of the deceased.

2. *The acquisitions of symptoms belonging to the last illness of the deceased.* Depression, imagination, and other psychological conditions influence this development. The extent of their influence cannot always be established with certainty.

3. *Sometimes a medically recognizable disease develops.* It has been noticed that the occurrence of malignancy is considerably higher in persons who were recently bereaved.

4. *The relationship with family and friends changes.* The bereaved person may become very irritable or may avoid former friends; sometimes they antagonize them deliberately.

5. *The bereaved may develop a furious hostility toward a specific person,* often toward the doctor or nurse or surgeon. It is a kind of defensive mechanism so that they don't have to face a weakness or limitation in themselves or in their immediate relatives.

There are many other possible (distorted) expressions of grief. In extreme cases the grieving person may attempt suicide.

Among the factors that influence the nature or degree of grief, Theresa Rando[25] enumerates:

1. The quality of the relationship that is severed. It may be important to see whether the bereaved person suffers a "role loss," i.e., the loss of a function such as a husband or wife, or whether it is the loss of an "object or person."

2. The coping behavior and the coping ability of the bereaved.

3. Past experiences of grief or loss. A recent accumulation of losses may cause a special presence or absence of strength.

4. Cultural or ethnic background may increase or suppress the expression of grief.

5. The sex role, i.e., men may not be allowed to grieve.

6. The characteristics of the deceased and his or her function in the life of the mourner.

7. Unfinished business between deceased and bereaved.

8. The degree to which death was preventable.

These examples serve to show that grief touches the total human condition, and that the personality traits of the individual play a role in the form and intensity of grief.

Various Kinds of Grief

The symptoms of grief are usually clearly present in the acute grief process that results from a sudden loss. They appear in different degrees in other forms of grief also. Dr. Wayne E. Oates[26] discusses several forms of grief, all of which have something in common and yet, are also different and ask for varying responses. An understanding of these forms is important in the pastoral ministry because grief is a process of adaptation to life in a new situation that arises after a significant loss. Pastoral ministry must be supportive in this process.

Hope for resurrection and reward for suffering, views on possible communication with the dead, on reincarnation, or on total annihilation, play a role in a person's approach to grieving. All these factors enter into the process and place their demands on the minister's sensitivity. Christian hope (in an afterlife) is a major source of strength in coping with serious losses. However, in the struggle to develop and nourish this hope, elements of doubt will be part of the developmental stages through which the bereaved person must journey.

Anticipatory grief. Anticipatory grief is the struggle to come face to face with a loss that undoubtedly will change one's life. Anticipatory grief is not the pain of a past loss. It may be the fear for a future loss and its demands for necessary adaptation, or it can be the experience of a loss that the bereaved has not yet fully accepted. The individual is not alone in this struggle. Family and friends are around and play their role in the process. From the beginning to the final completion of this process several steps occur. Oates calls these steps "rituals" in which the interaction between the individual and his or her surrounding unfolds itself.

1. *The rituals of urging.* Family and friends encourage the patient into certain forms of behavior such as "Take it easy" or "Go and see a doctor." The patient is faced with the dilemma to remain independent or to give in and become dependent on others with the consequent possibility of loss of dignity.

2. *The rituals of diagnosis.* Getting a doctor's appointment is for some people a frightening experience, particularly when there seems to be reason to expect a serious illness. The unfamiliarity with medical procedures, medical equipment, and medical language contributes to the mysterious nature

of the experience. For such people it is important to meet a doctor who explains well and is understanding, or to meet others who can offer understanding and guidance.

3. *The rituals of resistance.* It is in this area that the five stages of grief as developed by Dr. Elizabeth Kuebler-Ross[27] may be understood. There is (a) *denial* that such a thing can happen to this person. There is (b) *anger.* This person is not allowed to be ill. It is a blow to the patient's own dignity and to the persons for whom he or she is responsible. This condition cannot be in accordance with the will of the loving God in whom the patient believes.

In view of the undeniable reality, the patient tries to (c) *bargain* with God, offering change of life or special services in exchange for health. When bargaining seems ineffective (d) a state of *depression* may take over in which the patient feels rejected by God and there seems to be a loss of all sense of personal value. It looks like an attitude of fatalism wherein all personal efforts seem futile. Finally the patient comes to grips with the situation (e) by either positively or negatively *accepting* his or her condition and making the best of it.

These stages do not necessarily occur in this order. Some seem not to occur at all or to be totally absorbed into other stages. Sometimes they may reverse. At other times there is a fluctuation when the patient goes back and forth between two or more stages. It is important to avoid categorization according to stages. Alertness and openness are essential for the minister, together with a sensitivity to allow the patient to work through the feelings of that moment.

4. *The rituals of family gathering and leave-taking.* This ritual refers more to the family than to the patient. Family members may need this time to express their own feelings that could not be expressed before, to repair broken relationships, or to affirm positive experiences. These moments are very important for leave-taking. The statement that such

feelings are painful for the patient is usually an invalid excuse. The pain that this may cause to the patient is in almost all instances mixed with joy and consolation because it takes him or her out of the isolation where illness tends to imprison a person.

5. *The rituals of prolongation.* Medical technology makes it possible to prolong human life. Sometimes it merely extends the actual process of dying. Either the patient or the family may be faced with very difficult decisions. The difference is very subtle. Prolongation of life may be understood either as the maintenance of human abilities in the current state of being, or as a return to a state of better human communication. Extending the process of dying may be understood as slowing down the irreversible process without any hope for improvement or even maintenance of the present condition. Many people see this approach as an affront to human dignity. There seems to be a growing tendency to prefer dying at home or in a hospice rather than in the "mechanical" surroundings of a hospital.

6. *The rituals of death vigil.* The approaching death usually places a heavy burden on the patient and on the family. Many hours are spent in waiting rooms. But praying and waiting have many different meanings. For some it is a time to pray for healing; for others it is a last chance to be present to a beloved person. The pastoral minister shows much of his or her care through briefings and interpretations. At the time of death, when relief is intermingled with pain and sorrow, a comforting presence is important.

   There are many other rituals that belong to the process of grieving, such as the *"notification of next of kin," "planning for the funeral and the funeral itself," "visiting the cemetery,"* and *"the division of effects."* All these aspects are part of the farewell to the loved one, and they contribute to the readjustment process of the bereaved to daily life. In cases where there is no death but a loss of health (loss of limb, incurable illness, etc.) the various rituals will be present in an adapted form. For the minister it is important to be keenly aware of the specific grief elements that are active in these circumstances.

Acute or traumatic grief. The major characteristic of acute grief is its sudden onset. There has been no time for preparation (anticipatory grief), and thus grief has a different meaning. The source and nature of suffering become important factors in determining the appropriate form of support to the patient and/or family. Traumatic grief is a more intense form of acute grief. It is a sudden onset which brings about a physical and emotional disorder. Major occurrences are likely to show themselves in:

1. *Physiological and psychological shock.* Sometimes a person may experience an acute physiological shock such as progressive circulatory failure that can cause damage to tissue. Blood circulation is incomplete, and this may cause lack of oxygen. In rare cases it may cause sudden death. The intervention of a physician is always required.

   In psychological shock a psychological numbness takes over. There may be a loss of meaning of life and action, loss of appetite, exhaustion, loss of the awareness of the religious meaning of life. God seems to have become a total stranger. This religious numbness is frequently accompanied by guilt for lack of confidence in God. The bereaved often sees no solution and fears that this feeling will continue forever. Sometimes it can be helpful to remind the bereaved that this condition will change and that even the desire for God is already a sign of faith in God and of God's presence.

2. *Sight and identification of the body.* This is another moment of intense grief that can cause physiological and psychological shock. Identification takes away the "if" or "perhaps" and brings home the harsh reality of the loss.

3. *Delayed reaction.* In some cases grief is delayed and the bereaved manage to keep themselves alert during the time of wake and funeral. They may break down more intensely thereafter.

Grief is a process that takes time. Its length can hardly be determined. It depends on the personality of the individuals. According to some experts, normal grief can extend itself over a period of two years. Often people say that time heals all wounds. I do not believe this. Time does not heal anything, but the human being needs time to heal him or her self. In the process of healing, pastoral involvement can be invaluable.

There are other forms of acute grief that occur with more or less frequency. For instance, when a series of mishaps happens to the same individual or family, or when a child is born with a physical or mental handicap, we speak of a *"no end grief."* The suddenness of the onset can make it an acute grief, but the prolonged nature of the condition that causes the grief places it in a special category of chronic human conditions which ask for a continuous adjustment of life, as in the birth of a handicapped child. Occasionally there is a *near-miss grief* when the expected loss does not occur. The individual was already so intensely adjusted to the loss that the recovery asks for a readjustment to life.

Acute grief can become pathological when either the intensity or the duration of the grief is out of proportion to its source. In such instances professional help will be necessary. Some of its characteristics have been mentioned earlier.

The healing profession itself is sometimes the subject of another kind of grief called the *"tragic sense of life."* The repeated and prolonged contact with chronic suffering, such as handicapped children, or AIDS patients, can cause a sadness in the helper that may look like depression but is, in fact, a grieving about the condition of humanity exemplified in the many persons they meet. The person who experiences this tragic sense of life needs a deep faith and a healing community in order to overcome the slowly debilitating influence of the sadness that has taken hold of him or her. (For more detailed studies on nature and forms of grief and on human reactions to it, one may read Rando: *Grief, Dying and Death,* p. 23 ff.)

ILLNESS IN INTERHUMAN PERSPECTIVE

On face value it may seem as if an illness affects only the one individual who is ill with cancer or any other disease. However, the illness of one person affects many other people, particularly the members of the family. In daily human life we are all dependent upon other people. Husbands and wives depend on each other in many ways. Children depend on parents and parents on children. Children depend on each other. Consciously or unconsciously every family develops a division of roles to assure a certain regularity and balance in daily life. This role division is seriously interrupted when one member of the family falls ill.

As long as an illness is minor or of short duration, it is relatively easy to take on extra burdens. Often it is a joy to help others when they need assistance. In serious illness or in long protracted suffering, the situation is more complicated. Other members of the family cannot absorb extra burdens forever, however much they may love the sick person. If the breadwinner falls ill, or must stay home to take care of a sick child, the home situation changes significantly.

In order to evaluate the readjustments that need to be made in these circumstances, certain points of information are very important. Here are a few of these:

How important are physical health and bodily integrity for this person? Obviously, the loss of bodily integrity is always a traumatic experience, but the loss of a finger is more damaging to a pianist than to a farmer, and the loss of a leg is more traumatic for a long distance runner than for a person who spends most of his or her time at a desk. In some persons the self-image is closely related to bodily integrity. A scar on the face has more effect on the self-image of the beauty queen than of the coalminer. All these factors influence the process of adjustment.

What is the place of the individual in the family relationship? The illness of the breadwinner or the housekeeper will affect the family differently than the illness of a child. The sick bread-winner may develop guilt feelings for not being able to fulfill his or her duties. Accordingly, readjustment will be more diffi-cult to achieve.

Sometimes illness provides secondary gains. Being the center of attention, getting one's wishes fulfilled, or self-pity are attrac-tive to many people. Self-pity may be a pleasurable experience for the individual. These circumstances can have a great influ-ence upon the adjustment process. If the sick person is one of the children, other questions present themselves:

1. What is the place of this child in the family? Even if all chil-dren are deeply loved, each child has his or her own place in the family's favors and feelings.

2. How is the social life of the parents affected by the necessi-ty to stay at home and care for the child? How is their mutual relationship affected by the illness? The need for round-the-clock care, for example, can seriously infringe upon their time for intimacy and conversation.

3. How are the other children affected by the illness of one? They may receive less attention and have more chores.

4. How does the attitude of parents, brothers, and sisters affect the sick child? A sick child often goes through psychologi-cal changes such as developing guilt feelings or becoming demanding or manipulative.

These and many other questions are part and parcel of pain and suffering in the human experience. It is the pastoral minister's task to support not only the patient but also the family who is inseparably connected with the illness. The minister needs to have a deep sense of understanding and empathy without losing the necessary objectivity and without being blinded by manipulative behavior.

Suffering and
healing are essential
perspectives in the
life and teaching
of Jesus... It is
particularly the
redemptive element
of suffering that is
of the highest
importance.

CHAPTER FOUR

Pain and Suffering:
Biblical Teaching and Perspectives

Pain and suffering are concrete, undeniable, and unavoidable human experiences. They are also experiences that escape human understanding and baffle human intelligence. Their pervasive nature and ultimate source go so far beyond human insights that they often are attributed to mysterious if not divine influences. Ancient civilizations spoke about wars between gods, the dual principles of good and evil, human ignorance, and so on.[28] Some of the ancient writings seem to consider the condition of suffering a mandate to search for the restoration of human wholeness. Early Hindu compositions tell us that:

> through primeval ignorance human beings have made two fatal mistakes: first, they have taken the phenomenal world, that is, the world apprehended by the senses, as reality; and secondly, they cling to existence in this world, believing that they are individual persons or selves. But behind this phenomenal world is the true Reality (or Brahman) which is the source of all being. By clinging to the phenomenal world as reality and involving themselves with it, human beings become subject to a ceaseless process of birth and death, with all its consequent pain and suffering.[29]

To escape from this process one must engage in vigorous mental and physical discipline to achieve detachment from the desire to live in this phenomenal world.

The Judeo-Christian approach to the understanding of pain and suffering follows a similar route. It bases itself on creation narratives in which the devil destroyed existing peace, happiness, and wholeness by playing into the human need for independence and personal greatness. Disobedience deserves punishment and again a combination of human failure and divine activity (justice) form the source of pain and suffering.

For people who believe in God there is always a relationship between suffering and divine power. How these terms of the relationship influence each other can be seen in the development of religious understanding and in the progress (or retrogression) of human civilization. My present focus is on the religious understanding of pain and suffering as this is found in the biblical writings. The Bible as the Word of God is not only a place where God tells humanity about himself; it also gives basic outlines for human behavior in its relationship with God. The Bible tells us much about pain and suffering.

PAIN AND SUFFERING IN THE OLD TESTAMENT[30]

An understanding of suffering can be approached in many different ways. For our purpose I divide them into two broad areas. One deals with suffering that is experienced *by* the community or *for* the community. The other deals with suffering of individuals and its integration into personal life. Both areas search for the place of suffering in the life of the community and of the individual. From this perspective I will discuss three prominent themes in the Old Testament understanding of suffering:

1. The role of suffering *in the community* of the Chosen People.

2. The experience of *personal* pain and suffering.

3. The *religious meaning* of suffering.

The Role of Suffering in the Community of the Chosen People

God intervened frequently in the history of ancient Israel. Genesis speaks about this intervention in the call of Abraham (Gn. 12:1), the first covenant (Gn. 15:1 ff), the birth of Isaac (Gn. 21:1), Jacob's dream (Gn. 18:13), and at many more occasions. All these instances, however, describe a relationship between God and an individual, not an organized or communal religion. Israel's organized religion began when God appeared to Moses in the burning bush and said:

> I have witnessed the affliction of my people in Egypt and I have heard their cry of complaint against their slave-drivers, so I know well that they are suffering. Therefore I have come down to rescue them from the hands of the Egyptians and lead them out of that land into a good and spacious land ...(Ex. 3:7).

Thus at the beginning of Israel's organized religion lies the suffering of a people to whom God was present and whom he called "my people." This is also the people who had "cried out to God" against their oppressors and to whom God had decided to grant liberation. God, Yahweh, presents himself as a God who lives among them full of compassion and saving power. However, this compassionate and saving God asks for constant recognition and obedience. His authority is unquestioned.

This same God who is a "source of strength" is also the object of worship. Thus we read: "As Moses entered the tent where the column of cloud would come down ...all the people would rise and worship" (Ex. 33:9–10). After Moses spoke with the Lord, he had to draw a veil over his face, which was radiant with the splendor of the sacred word he had received (Ex. 34:29–35). Later, in establishing the covenant, God says of himself:

> I, the Lord, am your God who brought you
> out of the land of Egypt, that place of slavery
> (Ex. 20:2; Deut. 5:6).

God's power was experienced in the delivery from suffering. The same divine power also called for atonement for sinfulness.

Suffering through war and oppression. Many ancient religions portrayed God as a lofty and powerful being to whom they attributed the highest possible degree of all human qualities that they admired and desired. Their Gods were created by "human dreams." The Jewish religion, however, seems to originate from a concrete human reality and need. In the struggle for existence, and in the violence of war, the people sought divine protection and accepted divine leadership. Later this same divine leadership is transferred into daily life in which the Lord was seen as the guide and protector. One of the most common titles for Yahweh is "the God of Hosts" or the "Lord, mighty in battle." The psalmist expresses this in the words:

> Who is the King of Glory?
>   The Lord, strong and mighty,
>   The Lord mighty in battle ...
> Who is the King of Glory?
>   The Lord of Hosts (Ps. 24:8–10).

This reliance on God seems secular in origin, but it is worthwhile to notice that the "Lord of Hosts" also takes a prominent place in religious celebrations. The connection between secular and religious power is already visible in Egypt where Moses pronounces the punishment of the liberating God, while Aaron, the priest, performed the ritual action through which the punishment came down upon the land (Ex. 7:17–18, 24). On the journey through the desert, whenever the Ark of the Covenant was set out, Moses would pray, "Arise, O Lord, that your enemies may be scattered, and those who hate you may flee before you" (Ex. 10:35; Ps. 68:1). Deliverance and battle were inseparably connected. Both battle and deliverance are portrayed in the worship of the God who won the battle and who brought freedom.

Liturgical celebrations are an essential component in the Old Testament understanding of suffering. Many historical events, which may have had a much greater social impact than the Exodus, were not recorded. The departure of Israel from Egypt, however, made the leap from oral to written history. The primary reason for this is that it remained alive in the liturgical celebrations of the people.

Many religious celebrations, particularly the Passover, were a re-living of the liberating actions of Yahweh. The departure from Egypt never became merely a historical happening. It remained an ever-present reality and witness of Yahweh's love and protection. Thus the suffering and pain of war was at the same time a source of constant union with God. From the pain of war and oppression the Chosen People developed an understanding of a protecting and loving God whom they were called to worship in daily life.

Psychological suffering: waiting for the promise to be fulfilled. The Bible teaches us another form of pain and suffering that is not directly related to war and oppression. It is the psychological suffering of waiting. Waiting for the promise to be fulfilled lies at the heart of Israel's history. Abraham left his homeland to go to a foreign country waiting for his descendants to take possession of the promised land (Ex. 12:1). The Israelites wandered in the desert for forty years waiting for the fulfillment of the promise made to them. Even though this is marked by frequent and open rebellions against God, it was still a time carried by the hope that Yahweh would ultimately keep his promise.

After Israel entered into the promised land, all received the security of sharing in the tribal property (of land), except the priestly tribe of Levi, which had to rely on the gifts that came from the acts of worship. As the representatives of Yahweh among the people, they lived a "homeless" existence awaiting the fulfillment of the promise of Yahweh (Num. 8:16–18; Deut. 21:15–17; Judg. 17:7–9; 19:11). It is the lifestyle that St. Paul later will describe as the "vision of things unseen" (1 Cor. 4:16–18). *Waiting is a form of suffering that emphasizes human inadequacy and the need for total dependence on God.*

Sometimes the suffering of waiting was connected with violence of war and oppression. The Babylonian Exile serves as an example. It ruined Israel's comfortable existence and reduced it to a state of (semi) slavery. The Israelites had to wait for the end of their punishment, while in the meantime, the prophet of consolation (Is. 40) is sent to give them encouragement and support for their hope in the fulfillment of Yahweh's promise.

In this suffering, oppression and waiting are combined and there is also the promise of redemption and a new exodus (Is. 43:17). The central thought of this new exodus is the presence of Yahweh in all circumstances of life. "Should you pass through the water, I will be with you; in the rivers, you shall not drown" (Is. 43:2); "...Fear not for I am with you" (Is. 43:5). The unity of Yahweh with his people reaches such a height that Yahweh seems to enter into their suffering, as the prophet says, "You did not buy me sweet cane for money ..., instead you burdened me with your crimes. It is I, I who wiped out for my own sake your offenses" (Is. 43:24–25). Through the prophet, Yahweh indicates how deep the union between him and his people has grown because of their suffering and hope. In their own tribulation the Israelites hear the voice of the suffering God. Caroll Stuhlmueller says:

> If Israel sensed this blending of voices of suffering, her own and God's, then a mystic aura must have pervaded the suffering. Voices of contemplative prayer are merging with voices of suffering (*Voice of Suffering* ...p. 114).

The strength of Israel's hope is based upon God's fidelity in the past: "See the earlier things have come to pass, new ones

I now foretell; before they spring into being I announce them to you" (Is. 42:9). The presence of Yahweh pervades all existence as the prophet says: "Listen to me Jacob, Israel whom I named! I it is who am the first, and also the last am I. Yes, my hand laid the foundations of the earth; my right hand spread out the heavens" (Is. 48:12–13). Yahweh is the continuous support (source) of all that exists.

Although the community is suffering, the emphasis begins to shift to individual persons who are caught in this condition. What is said of the people in general is in a particular way realized in the person of the prophet. A prophet expresses in his or her life the suffering that will come to the nation. Thus the prophet's suffering is representative of the suffering of the people. It reveals God's anger and shows that suffering is the manner by which punishment will be carried out.

There is a special form of suffering when prophets, called and sent by God, were not accepted or were even rejected by the very people to whom they were sent. This happened to the prophets throughout the Old Testament. They suffered on account of the people and, in a certain way, it was through their suffering that the people received Yahweh's message of anger, forgiveness, and mercy. In certain instances the suffering of the prophet became an atonement for others. This finds profound and moving expression in the Songs of the Suffering Servant.

Suffering of atonement. Although physical suffering, through violence and oppression and psychological suffering of waiting and hoping, led to trust and union with God, much more intimate is the union between God and his servant in the spiritual suffering that took place in the fulfillment of his mission for others. The Servant Songs are the most complete example of this form of suffering. Four separate steps or stages can be distinguished, which together present a wholeness and totality of self-giving.

The first step is when *Yahweh introduces the servant* and states his qualities of fidelity, gentleness, and care (Is. 42:1–4). The servant's mission is well defined. He is called to manifest the victory of justice, to be a covenant of the people, and to bring relief to all who suffer (Is. 42:6–7).

The prophet describes the qualities of true service and creative presence. These qualities are inherent in human life and dignity, yet they are totally God's gifts. The service that is rendered is the manifestation of God's mercy made visible in the servant.

In the second step *the servant presents himself as being sent by Yahweh,* called from birth, frustrated in the fulfillment of his task, but undaunted in the service of God (Is. 49:1–6). The servant almost begs the people to listen because it is God who speaks through him. We hear his human discouragement; he fears that he has toiled in vain, but at the same time there is a recognition of total dependence on God. His personal confidence is unshaken because of the awareness of the mission that God has given him.

In the third step *the servant tells about the sufferings he has endured because of his mission,* but he also displays an unshaken confidence in God (Is. 50:4–9a).

In the fourth step it is again *Yahweh who speaks and describes the suffering of the servant as well as the servant's union with God* (Is. 52:13; 53:1–12).

Although the Songs of the Suffering Servant are usually applied to Christ, they also reflect the reality of human (Christian) life. Human life is a gift received from God for the purpose of manifesting God's love. Human creative development includes suffering and struggle, but ultimately there is a fulfillment in God.

The Old Testament portrays the interaction between physical, psychological, and spiritual suffering. Ultimately these three conditions interlock and place the total human reality in relationship to God.

Personal Pain and Suffering in the Bible[31]

The Bible presents many different kinds of personal suffering. The pain and struggles of the Chosen People were lived by individuals. The Book of Job is an outstanding example of a painful, personal experience of suffering.

The word for "suffering" that is used in the Old Testament has a general meaning of "that which is evil" and refers to physical as well as to moral evil. It names what is vicious or harmful.

There seems not to be a word that expresses the general concept of physical pain, but there is frequent reference to physical experiences which are known to be painful. These experiences are used to indicate human conditions of suffering. For instance: *birth pangs* as a human experience of pain is also used to indicate anguish that is general, unavoidable, and severe; *shuddering and quaking* of the body is seen as the result of torment of pain, anguish, or fear; *vexen and sullen* is understood as a condition of a deep suffering; *mourning* reflects an especially difficult human situation. Thus, physical suffering is viewed as an expression and representation of psychological experiences, while psychological suffering is portrayed in physical images. In all circumstances, however, suffering is an experience of the whole human being and is not limited to either psychic or physical organisms. This is conveyed in several poignant stories in Scriptures.

Anguish in confrontation with death affects the total person. We see this in Hezikiah's fear of dying (2 Kings 20:1 ff), in Hagar's agony when she had to leave her child to die in the desert (Gn. 21:15 ff), and in Jacob's sorrow when he was told of Joseph's disappearance (Gn. 37: 31 ff). Indelibly painful was the death of a first born child or of an only son (Jer. 6:26; Zech. 12:10).

Loneliness did not only affect the emotional life but the whole human person, as we see in the fear of childlessness in Abraham (Gn. 15:2) and Hannah (1 Sam. 1:9 ff). We encounter throughout the Psalms the pain of homesickness and the inability to worship in freedom.

Experience of rejection became a source of anger and bitterness with life. Unfaithfulness of friends became an unbearable burden that affected behavior and could cause physical illness.

The Old Testament persons did not try to deny pain or hide from it. They were not afraid to show their suffering by lamenting and weeping, yet they displayed an attitude of tolerance or asceticism that led them to accept the inevitable. Without understanding the source or the total purpose of suffering, they did incorporate it into their relationship with God.

The Religious Meaning of Suffering[32]

The Old Testament identifies the ultimate source of suffering as a disturbance in the human relationship with God. The story of the Fall testifies that when the anger of God was incurred, humanity suffered. Child-bearing and food-gathering became hardships (Gn. 3:16–19), and finally, a disturbance in the relationship with God was the cause of death. Death was the work of the devil as is stated in Wisdom 2:24: "…by the envy of the devil death entered into the world, and they who are in his possession experience it."

Although there was an involvement of God in human suffering and much of the suffering was attributed to sin, there were many other circumstances that played a role in this human condition. Frequently suffering was a cause for alienation from God and made individuals question God's wisdom and love. Quite often suffering also brought people closer to God. Let us now look at the Old Testament religious meaning of suffering from these two opposite perspectives.

Seemingly disadvantageous consequences of suffering. Some circumstances of life appear to be utterly incomprehensible, unreasonable, and unjust. Many people who disregard God's law thrive while others who obey God's law suffer hardship. The psalmist speaks about this in Psalm 73: "The wicked are sound and sleek…they are free from the burdens of mortals…" (v. 4–5), but the just "suffer affliction day after day…" (v. 14). Suffering makes them "almost lose their balance…" (v. 2).

To make matters worse, being in the service of God often invites suffering. Moses, the servant sent by God (Ex. 4: 1 ff), came to such a state of frustration on account of the rebellious attitude of the people, that he questioned the justice of bringing forth water from the rock (Num. 20:10 ff). On many occasions the prophets asked God to relieve them of their mission or even to take their life because their suffering became so unbearable. (See Is. 49:4; 50:6; 52:13; 53:12. Jer. 1:8; 1:17 f.; 12:5 f.; 20:7–13. Ezek. 2:6; 24:15–18.)

At times of crisis suffering promoted doubt and temptation. Moses questioned the wisdom and justice of God when Pharaoh did not listen (Ex. 5:22) and when the Jews disobeyed (Num. 11:11). Joshua was angry with God when the country of the Amorites seemed unconquerable.

Jeremiah wanted to discuss a few things with God (Num. 12:1) and posed several questions (15:18). He went so far as to accuse God of having seduced him (20:7).

Job frequently expressed his anger with God as in 7:12; 9:22; 19:6–12; 30:17–22.

The intensity and depth of suffering could make the strongest persons doubt the wisdom of God and alienate many of lesser faith.

Religiously advantageous consequences of suffering. Although suffering was at times experienced as a factor that made the relationship with God more difficult to accept, it also acted as a catalyst for personal choice that bound humanity to God.

1. *Suffering compels a person to decide for or against God.* Any attraction to doubt or rejection is also an opportunity to make a decision toward faithfulness. The Scriptures give us many examples of those who made this choice. Here are but a few:

   God asked Abraham to sacrifice his only son (Gn. 22). Because of his faithfulness to Yahweh, he was blessed. Psalm 30 describes the beneficial effects of faithfulness to God throughout the suffering that was endured.

   In the book of Job (1:11) Satan is convinced that under the pressure of suffering Job will denounce God, certainly

when suffering touches his body and being (2:5). Job choos-
es otherwise.

2. *Suffering shakes a person out of his or her self-confidence,* opens
   the individual to the process of healing, and leads to recognition of God's presence and authority.

   God asks people to listen to his commands. Exodus
   15:26: "If you really listen to the voice of the Lord your
   God," he told them, "and you do what is right in his eyes;
   and if you heed his commandments and keep all his pre-
   cepts, I will not afflict you with any of the diseases with
   which I will afflict the Egyptians..."

   He warns them that he is the master of life and death.
   Deut. 32:39: "It is I who will govern both life and death, and
   I who inflicts wounds and heals them, and from my hand
   there is no rescue."

   The prophets point to God as the hand of both punishment and healing.

   Isaiah 19:22 (and 30:26): "Although the Lord shall smite
   Egypt severely, he shall heal them; they shall turn to the
   Lord, and he shall be won over and heal them."

   Jeremiah 31:19, speaking about the restoration of the
   Northern kingdom, says: "I return in repentance; I have
   come to myself, and I strike my breast."

   Hosea 6:1: "Come let us return to the Lord, for it is he
   who has rent, and he will heal us; he has struck us, but he
   will bind our wounds."

3. *Suffering is a form of chastisement, and it purifies devotion to
   God.* It is, therefore, not a vengeance but a help in the
   process of healing. God's mercy is never absent.

   Jeremiah 10:24 prays to God: "Punish us, O Lord, but
   with equity not in anger lest you have us dwindle away."
   Verses 30:11; 31:18; 46:28 speak about "discipline with mod-
   eration."

   Lamentations 3:32–33: "Though he punishes, he takes
   pity in the abundance of his mercies; he has no joy in afflict-

ing or grieving the sons of men."

Wisdom 3:5 praises the faithful: "Chastised a little, they shall be greatly blessed, because God tried them and found them worthy of himself. As gold in the furnace he proved them, and as sacrificial offerings he took them to himself."

Psalm 30 is a prayer of thanksgiving after mortal danger.

Psalm 31 is a prayer in time of ordeal.

Sirach 2:5: "For in fire gold is tested, and worthy men in the crucible of humiliation."

4. *Suffering leads to repentance and an acknowledgment of faults; it becomes a prompt to conversion.* This is a frequent theme in the Psalms.

Psalms 32:4–5: "For day and night your hand was heavy upon me. My strength was dried up as by the heat of summer. Then I acknowledged my sin to you, my guilt I covered not…"

Psalms 34:19: "The Lord is close to the broken-hearted; and those who are crushed in spirit he saves…"

Psalms 38 is a prayer of an afflicted sinner who comes back to Yahweh.

Psalms 51:19: "My sacrifice, O God, is a contrite spirit; a heart contrite and humbled, O God, you will not spurn."

5. *Suffering moves God to compassion and forgiveness.* Genesis 21:17: "God heard the boy's cry, and God's messenger called to Hagar from heaven: What is the matter Hagar? Don't be afraid; God has heard the boy's cry in this plight of his…"

Exodus 2:24: When God called Moses he said to him, "As their cry for release went up to God, he heard their groaning and was mindful of his covenant with Abraham, Isaac and Jacob…" (also 3:7).

2 Kings 20:5: God said to Isaiah "Go back and tell Hezekiah, the leader of my people: Thus says the Lord, the God of your forefather, David: I have heard your prayer and seen your tears. I will heal you …"; 22:19: "…because

you tore your garments and wept before me; I in turn have listened, says the Lord ..."

Tobit 3:16: "At that very time the prayer of these two supplicants (Tobit and Sarah) was heard in the glorious presence of the Almighty ..."

6. *Suffering brings reward from God.* In Genesis 22:16 Abraham was promised special blessings because of his obedience to God.

1 Samuel 2 gives the prayer of Hannah after the birth of Samuel.

2 Macchabees 7:11: One of the seven brothers said: "It was from heaven that I received these; for the sake of his laws I disdain them; from him I hope to receive them again ..."

7. *Suffering is a source of atonement.* Suffering not only serves the possibility of union with God for the individual who accepts it, it can also benefit others for whose sake it is endured. At no point in the Old Testament is this more clearly expressed than in the Songs of the Suffering Servant. The suffering of the servant was endured by the individual, but the people benefited from it in a special way.

We see the same belief in 2 Macchabean 7:37 where the youngest son said: "Like my brothers I offer up my body and my life for our ancestral laws, imploring God to show mercy soon to our nation, and by afflictions and blows to make you confess that he alone is God."

The characteristics of the Old Testament understanding of suffering may be summarized as follows:

1. The Old Testament accepts the reality of suffering as a dimension of human existence.

2. Suffering is never sought for its own sake but when it occurs, it is dealt with as an unavoidable aspect of life.

3. Suffering is not understood; people search for its meaning rather than its source.

4. The experience of suffering is beyond human control. Suffering finds its origin either in God or in Satan. It is always experienced as a disturbance in the harmony of human life.

5. When suffering comes from God, it can either come directly, or through human intervention. In all circumstances it draws the attention to God and asks for an amendment of life.

6. Suffering accepted in patience is a source of forgiveness and renewed friendship with God.

7. Suffering of the innocent and the just is an example for others to relinquish their sinful ways. Through the suffering of the innocent, God's mercy and compassion are aroused and protection is given.

The Old Testament considered suffering to be a deeply human experience that united the people with God if it was accepted and carried in faith. This perspective leads to the meaning of suffering in the New Testament.

PAIN AND SUFFERING IN THE NEW TESTAMENT

Jesus did not come to abolish the law and the prophets, but to bring them to fulfillment (Mt. 5:17). He was announced by John the Baptizer as: "The Lamb of God who takes away the sin of the world" (Jn. 1:29). In the Old Testament there was a close connection between human sinfulness and the relationship of Yahweh to his people. It is, therefore, not surprising that the role of suffering, as it existed in the Old Testament, carries over into the New—but with a dramatically altered perspective. John the Baptizer here points to the new relationship between sinfulness and the mission of Jesus.

The organized religion of the Old Testament was born as a response to the people's cry for relief from suffering and pain: "I have witnessed the affliction of my people and have heard their cry of complaint against their slave-drivers …(Ex. 3:7–10). So in the New Testament Jesus came in the fullness of time to fulfill the people's desire and expectation for reunion with God.

In many oriental religions the gods were glorious appearances, and worship was a celebration of majesty and splendor. In the early Jewish religion God came as the deliverer from slavery, and worship was a celebration of protective and redemptive power. Consequently, the experience of pain and suffering entered necessarily into their religious expressions because it was in pain and suffering that the human and the divine touched.

Christianity comes from an ancestry that incorporates misery and redemption, submission to slavery, and liberation. It contains within itself these same elements. The Messiah came to liberate and to redeem from sinfulness. Enslavement to sin existed in daily human life, and redemption came as a gift of God manifested in the human reality. The New Testament offers four prominent themes for our understanding of pain and suffering:

1. The search for the cause of suffering.

2. The suffering of Jesus in his daily life.

3. Suffering and the discipleship of Jesus.

4. The passion and death of Jesus.

The Search for the Cause of Suffering

The New Testament does not offer a definitive answer in the search for the "why" of suffering. However, the two major causes are indicated:

1. *The power of the devil* is occasionally indicated as a cause of suffering. This is stated in the story of the healing of the

crippled woman on the sabbath. Jesus freed the woman who had "been in the bondage of Satan for eighteen years" (Lk. 13:10–17). Paul endured temptations: "I was given a thorn in the flesh, an angel of Satan to beat me ...," in order to remain humble in the midst of revelations (2 Cor. 12–7).[33] In the Acts of the Apostles (10:38), Peter says that Jesus "... went about doing good works and healing all who were in the grip of the devil ..." The frequent driving out of evil spirits suggests that Satan was often seen as the cause of human suffering.

2. *Punishment for ill behavior* is another cause that occasionally surfaces as the origin of suffering. Jesus warns that: "... you will all come to the same end unless you reform"(Lk. 13:1–6). The possibility or even the prospect of suffering is a warning or a deterrent from sin for those who know what has happened to others before them. St. Paul also suggests that suffering can be a punishment. In relation to the Eucharist he says: "He who eats and drinks without recognizing the body eats and drinks a judgment on himself" (1 Cor. 11:29).

However, we must be very careful not to misunderstand the teaching of the Scriptures. Jesus warns explicitly that not all suffering is punishment, but in suffering and healing, one must be able to recognize the greatness and love of God. Jesus stated this clearly in the healing of the man who was born blind: "It was no sin either of this man or of his parents ..." (Jn 9–1 ff). The story of the poor Lazarus (Lk. 16:19–31) rejects the concept that suffering is always a retribution for sinfulness.

The Suffering of Jesus in his Daily Life[34]

Jesus was human in the full sense of the word. Although his life was continuously in the deepest union with the Father, he was also subject to all human limitations and experiences of physical and psychological stress. This human condition belongs to his messianic mission. The following points are of importance to the understanding of suffering in the life of Jesus as they reflect his sharing in the plight of all humanity.

1. *The experience of insecurity in human life.* Jesus had no home. He said: "The foxes have lairs, the birds in the sky have nests, but the Son of Man has nowhere to lay his head" (Mt. 8:20; Lk. 9:58).

2. *The loneliness of personal existence.* Jesus lived in a culture where family ties were very important, yet, he left his family behind and said: "Who are my mother and my brothers? ...Whoever does the will of God is brother and sister and mother to me" (Mk. 3:35).

   Jesus was not understood by his own people. The hostility of the religious leaders is evident throughout the gospels. He himself declared: "...no prophet gains acceptance in his native place ..." (Lk. 4:24).

3. *The demanding pressures of daily life.* The gospels speak about Jesus' exhaustion after traveling and preaching. Even when he tried to take necessary rest, people came to him, and he did not turn them away.

4. *The experience of apparent failures in work and mission.* Jesus was aware of his impending suffering and death. He told his followers that "...the Son of Man had to suffer much, be rejected by the elders, the chief priests and scribes, be put to death and rise three days later" (Mk. 8:31; 9:31; 10:33; 14:21; and Lk. 13:32 ff). It was a pressure he lived with constantly, but accepted (integrated as part of his life) as the will of the Father. He was called for the sake of others: "The Son of Man has not come to be served but to serve— to give his life in ransom for many" (Mk. 10:45). However, he embraced this condition as the only way to his glory: "Did not the Messiah have to undergo all this so as to enter into his glory?" (Lk. 24:26).

Suffering and the Discipleship of Jesus

Jesus never promised his disciples a rose garden. He made it very clear that they could expect trials and suffering, and that these were a part of discipleship. The disciple must "... deny himself, take up his cross, and follow in my footsteps" (Mk. 8:34). They were warned that "Whoever will save his life will lose it, but whoever loses his life for my sake and the gospel's will gain it" (Mk. 8:35; also Mt. 10:38; Lk. 14:27).

The nature of their suffering mirrored Jesus' suffering in his daily life. They, too, were subject to the same stresses:

1. *The insecurity of human life* in renouncing home and surroundings as Jesus told the scribe who wanted to follow him (Mt. 8:19).

2. *Changes in family relationship* as Jesus indicated when he said: "...I have come to set a man at odds with his father, a daughter with her mother, a daughter-in-law with her mother-in-law; in short, to make a man's enemies those of his own household" (Mt. 10:35–36).

   He asked them to be willing to suffer hatred and persecution when they were drawn before synagogues and rulers for the sake of his name (Mt. 13:1–13).

3. *They must make a choice for or against Jesus* even if it would cause discord in the family. "I have come to light a fire on earth...a household of five will be divided three against two and two against three..." (Lk. 12:49–53; also Mt. 10:34–36).

4. *Jesus demands abnegation and detachment in his service* even to the point of laying down one's life. Only when one loses one's life, can one save it (Mt. 8:35). It was stated again clearly in John 12:24: "I solemnly assure you, unless a grain of wheat falls to the earth and dies, it remains just a grain of wheat. But if it dies, it produces much fruit."

The Passion and Death of Jesus

The deep compassion that Jesus showed for the suffering of mankind and the many miracles of healing he performed reveal that alleviating suffering was one of the essential dimensions in his messianic mission. There is, however, a strange contradiction in the fact that at one moment he heals human suffering, and at the next moment he predicts suffering, and even death, for his followers.

The great emphasis on healing and the many miracles he worked may obscure the deeper meaning of Jesus' life and work. These miracles may give the impression that it was Jesus' purpose to eliminate suffering from this earth. If this were true, it would reduce or minimize the redemptive value of suffering. It would be a mistake to see the task of Jesus from the viewpoint of one aspect of life. One must constantly keep in mind the totality of Jesus' life and mission.

Suffering and healing are essential perspectives in the life and teaching of Jesus as well as in the life and teaching of his followers. It is particularly the redemptive element of suffering that is of the highest importance. The prophet Isaiah said: "By his stripes we are healed ..." (Is. 53:5). Jesus and his disciples shared in this redemptive suffering.

The Passion of Jesus. Earlier I have stated that some experiences of pain and suffering are meaningless. This is to say they indicate a severe threat to the organism, but they do not contribute as a warning that leads to a possibility for healing. For many people the passion of Jesus falls into this category. Peter had great difficulty accepting the necessity of Jesus' suffering. He remonstrated against it, but he was rebuked by Jesus (Mk. 8:31–33). St. Paul sums up a variety of opinions when he says: "...but we preach Christ crucified—a stumbling block to Jews, and an absurdity to the Gentiles; but to those who are called, Jews and Greek alike, Christ is the power of God and the wisdom of God" (1 Cor. 1:23–24). Elsewhere Paul appreciates the death of Jesus as an atonement for sins, but it is followed by the resurrection: "…Christ died for our sins in accordance with the scriptures; he was buried and, in accordance with the scriptures, he rose on the third day" (1 Cor. 15:3 ff.). However, we must not overlook the fact that Jesus' death led to resurrection because of the nature and meaning of Jesus' mission.

Earlier I mentioned the seeming contradictions when Jesus healed those who were afflicted and almost immediately predicts (even promises) suffering for those who are his followers. In his article "Human Suffering and the Passion of Christ,"[35] Arthur McGill points to three significant elements of the gospel accounts on Jesus' suffering:

1. *There is no hint in the gospel narratives that we may or should or must get rid of suffering.* Despite the many miracles of healing related by the evangelists, the entire New Testament is unanimous in connecting Christ's submission to suffering with his way of relating to God. There have been efforts to minimize the physical suffering of Jesus by saying that, as God, he was free from the imperfections of the human body, but all gospel evidence argues against that. His agony seems clear from his cry: "My God, My God, why have you forsaken me?"

2. *Jesus did not seek to remove himself from suffering.* He prayed to the Father to let the chalice pass by, but he was ready to accept the Father's will. He did not indicate in any way that he considered his suffering in itself as good or advisable. To be sure, we know from scriptural teaching that humanity is tested, disciplined, purged, and purified when it undergoes suffering (2 Cor. 6:9; Heb. 12:6–11), but this purification is not the result of suffering as such. Rather, it depends on the acceptance of one's human life and human condition as an invitation of God.

3. *The gospel accounts of the Passion project little or no hope for reward in the face of suffering.* Jesus does not seem to rely on the beneficial outcome or results of his suffering. He is

totally immersed in the pain, which had no prospect on its own merits. Yet, it is precisely at this point that the deepest meaning of his suffering comes to the fore. This can perhaps best be learned from the words of Jesus: "Father, into your hands I commend my spirit" (Lk. 23:46). According to McGill, these words can be understood in two different ways.

First, there is the "weak" meaning in which a person (Christ) commends to the Father all his hopes, values, and expectations with the confidence that the Father will take care of them. It is the point of human surrender at which a person is helpless and powerless, yet expects to come through the difficulties on account of reliance on God. It is an attitude that still maintains the hope and expectation of a human solution, though it be through God's intervention.

Second, there is the "strong" meaning in which the individual is fully aware of total and complete helplessness. All human support systems have fallen away. Even the confidence in God's intervention seems to have gone (My God, why have you forsaken me?). Yet, in an act of full human consciousness, Christ commends himself to God as the ultimate source of good who deserves his total dedication.

In this context the suffering of Jesus becomes the living expression of total human consecration to the Father. All physical, psychological, and even religious support systems on the human level have ceased to function. In this state of absolute emptiness Jesus expresses his entire surrender to the one who sent him. In his human reality, Jesus at this moment ascended above the material and any other limitation that could stand between human dedication and God, in order to surrender his total being to the Father. It was the supreme moment of redemption in which the power of flesh and sin was overcome and humanity gave itself completely into God's hands. Sin was conquered. Nothing stood between God and the human. Therefore, at the moment that Jesus died, he also entered into the resurrection. This "strong" meaning is not a passive "letting go" into the hands of God, but an active and positive self-giving of his life into the hands of the Creator. Jesus accepted his death in obedience to the Father: "...but let it be as you would have it, not as I" (Mk. 14:36), and "...it was thus that he humbled himself, obediently accepting even death, death on a cross!" (Phil. 2:8). The surrender upon the cross was the final act of obedience in which all reliance on created human life and human condition was effectively and completely overcome.

This supreme act of obedience was also the moment in which Jesus *as human* was most vulnerable. All the walls that protect human existence had fallen away. His commitment to the Father was the final, most complete actualization of his humanity. It was the full recognition that he was placed in this world for uncompromising service of God without fear or reservation and without being limited by any aspect of the human condition. Thus Jesus' supreme suffering was also the exquisite freeing act of fulfillment, which ultimately can only be grasped in an act of faith. God raised him up and made him the first among the living in response to this absolute and total self-giving to the Father (Acts 2:23; 3:13–18; Rom. 4:25; 8:32). This supreme act of surrender was also the revelation of the goal of human existence, namely, to journey through the material to arrive at full freedom from the material in total surrender to God. It reveals the ultimate meaning of suffering: the progressive detachment from material conditions toward full spiritual freedom.

Discipleship and the Passion of Jesus. Just as this highest act of obedience gave meaning to all the suffering and continuous detachment in the life of Jesus until it culminated in utter commitment to the Father, so it also outlined the course and meaning of the life of the disciples. The disciples had to suffer *because* of their discipleship of Jesus, and *because* they do not belong to this world, although they are in it (Jn. 17:11). The essence of discipleship lies in that form of obedience in which detachment from the world unites them with God without taking them out of the world.

St. Paul maintains that "Anyone who wants to live a godly existence in Christ can expect to be persecuted" (2 Tim. 3:12), but Christ will be the ultimate source of hope and security (2 Tim 1:12). Paul considers it a badge of distinction to suffer with Christ ". . . for it is your special privilege to take Christ's part—not only to believe in him but also suffer for him" (Phil. 1:29), and he is ready to shed his own blood if necessary (Phil. 2:17).

Paul reminds his followers that in fact all believers have to suffer (Acts 14:22) and he gives examples of his own experience for the church of Macedonia (2 Cor. 8:2). Suffering was also the way God kept him from pride in his revelations (2 Cor. 12:7). He considers suffering an honor, for through it he makes up in his own body what is still to be undergone by Christ for the sake of his body the Church (Col. 1:24). He finds comfort in his faith in Christ (2 Cor. 7:6). He feels pride for the believers who suffer with courage (2 Thess. 1:3–4). He prays that the Lord may give them strength (2 Thess. 3:3). He hopes that his suffering may not be a source of discouragement for others (Eph. 3:13).

Suffering is inseparably connected to the discipleship of Jesus, not for the sake of suffering, but as a human necessity to rise above the material toward a surrender to God. To be a Christian means to die and live with Christ so that God be glorified in all.

God does not want
humanity to suffer but
to integrate suffering
into the totality of life
in service of God.

CHAPTER FIVE

Pain and Suffering:
Search for Theological Understanding

Suffering is such a deeply personal reality and general experience that we cannot realistically imagine human existence without some form of it. Because humanity is created in the image of God, it is understandable that people have seen some sort of relationship between God and the human encounter with pain and suffering. Scriptures suggest this relationship. Judeo-Christianity had its origin in the experience of suffering. "Yahweh saw the affliction of his people and heard their cry." (See Ex. 3:7) Jesus came to obtain redemption and forgiveness for our sins. Both the affliction of the Jewish people and the sinfulness of humanity indicate suffering. Both call forth a liberating and redeeming action of God. In this context the question arises "What is the cause of suffering?" and "Why does a loving and redeeming God who heals the suffering allow it to happen in the first place?"

Suffering is very personal. It is an experience that touches the deepest and innermost strivings of each individual. It can hinder the achievement of human wholeness and strike at the core of the human being. The questions "Why?" and "Why me?" are more than intellectual curiosity. Consciously or unconsciously humanity knows itself dependent on a power beyond its control (God) and called to search for personal wholeness. The experience of pain and suffering seems incomprehensible. Humanity searches for a solution to how an individual can give

a meaningful expression to his or her life in the present circumstances. Every human search for health contains the desire
to maintain or improve one's present condition or to restore
life to its former (familiar) shape. The "why?" and "why me?"
are not merely questions *about* suffering; they also contain a
search for an integration of the experience of suffering with the
goal of life as this is known from one's talents and circumstances of life.

Theological reflections on suffering cannot give a satisfac-
tory answer. In the presence of suffering, more often than not
one can only remain silent in empathy and compassion. The
deep, individual pain cannot be alleviated by abstract reasoning. Yet, as Gisbert Greshake says in his article "Human Suffering and the Question of God":

> ...precisely because suffering must be per-
> sonally and existentially overcome, and since
> reflective thinking forms a vital mode of
> personal existence, theology must occupy
> itself with the question: "along which lines
> must pain be understood, so that it can be
> existentially subsumed and integrated?"
> While a theory of suffering is not by itself
> an adequate solution, it can give the frame-
> work within which the solution is to be
> sought.[36]

Obviously, the most important source for the formation of
human attitudes toward suffering is found in the Scriptures, in
the Old Testament as well as the New Testament, and in the life
and teachings of Jesus. We have studied these teachings briefly
in the previous chapter. Here I want to reflect on what human
reasoning and understanding can tell us about the relationship
between suffering and God.

INADEQUATE EFFORTS TO UNDERSTAND SUFFERING

Since time immemorial humanity has searched for ways to explain the phenomenon of suffering—usually with little success. In his article "The Mystery of Injustice and the Mystery of Mercy"[37] Edward Schillebeeckx lists the frequently used efforts to find an answer for the origin of suffering. The experience of pain and suffering in human life seems to be in direct opposition to the concept of a loving and caring God. Most explanations try to lend a rationale to suffering while retaining a belief in God's goodness. None of the explanations, however, is adequate. Here are some examples:

1. A *dualistic explanation* accepts a double first principle; one is the principle of good, the other is the principle of evil. How the origin and power of such totally opposite principles can be explained is not mentioned. Thus the uncertainty remains.

2. Later efforts have been made to explain *suffering as non-being* in the sense that it ought not to be. This approach does not consider evil to be its own independent (inexplicable) principle; it does not explain its origin and reason either. It emphasizes that suffering and evil cannot be understood but it does not explain why not.

3. *Stoicism* envisioned the world as mysteriously integrated, including the presence of suffering and pain. The existing world is the *best possible* world, and for the stoics there was always the possibility of deliberate suicide if life became too difficult. This approach does not explain the origin and reason of suffering. Even the argument that the world is good, and that the occurrence of evil is only superficial but that in final analysis all works for the good, does not solve the question. Suffering is a reality and we don't know why.

4. Another approach states that *God allows evil and suffering to occur in view of the good that can follow from it.* This is an assumption that cannot be proven and does not explain any source or reason for suffering. Furthermore, it places in God himself a conflict of wanting an absolute good and yet using evil to achieve it.

5. In a secularized society where God is, at best, on the periphery of being, the blame for suffering and evil is placed on the *human being*. People themselves interfere with the course of nature; create circumstances that lead to accidents; gather in one place and cause large numbers to die in earthquakes, floods, and so on. However, blaming does not provide an explanation. Even when human beings are responsible for evil, there still remains the question "What enables them and what gives them the will to do so and what causes the accident or disaster?"

6. If God remains in the picture, and the blame is given to *Adam and Eve or to the devil,* the problem remains equally unsolved. Where did they get the power? The question of the origin of evil and suffering remains unanswered.

As long as the "why" question of suffering is understood as a *search for a solution* to the problem of suffering, we are bound to miss the point. Suffering is not an abstract reality that can be applied to people and that, therefore, can be solved by reasoning and understanding. Humanity "undergoes" suffering, and answers "about" suffering will not provide any solution. Theological knowledge and human experience are different realms of being. Greshake points out that:

> Whatever anyone proffers upon the problem of suffering really changes nothing. If we observe carefully, we will notice that reflections upon suffering generally arise not from the arena of suffering but rather from the tri-

bunes. Down in the arena people suffer, perhaps amid complaints and cries of distress;
maybe all this time they praise God, but they
scarcely reflect upon their suffering. In the
painful arena, suffering is not a problem; it is
a reality.[38]

Notice that Greshake says that suffering is not a problem
that asks for a solution, but a reality that needs to be integrated into life.

Despite the inadequacy of all these efforts and the fact
that theoretical knowledge and experience are two different
realms of being, it is nevertheless appropriate to continue to
search for an answer to the question "why?" This is not merely a reaching out to discover an intellectual response to the
question of the origin of suffering. It is primarily a search for
an understanding that can offer a framework within which
attitudes can be formed and directions for a response to suffering can be formulated. This is the task I have taken up in the
following pages.

SUFFERING: A QUALITY INHERENT TO CREATION

Creation as we know it is in a state of constant development. The transition from one state to another includes a tension in which the natural striving to maintain a status quo is in
conflict with the necessary unfolding of other innate qualities.
These transitions include a form of suffering. Suffering is not
the same as having pain. Suffering presupposes a brain function that provides both awareness and a certain form of knowledge. It includes a knowledge of what one can do (or is
supposed to be able to do) and the conscious experience of not
being able to act in accordance with one's "call" or "wish." It
is, therefore, difficult to speak of suffering in the world of
organic matter or in the world of plants. From a certain point
of view, it is even difficult to speak of suffering in the world
of animals.

Suffering, in its fullest meaning, belongs to the human world. Humans are aware of discomfort, that certain functions are hindered, and that potentials and goals cannot be fulfilled. In this encounter, human persons suffer consciously. A human being is part of the whole cosmic reality and is touched by and conscious of the material changes that take place. In addition, human beings add to the changes through personal activity. This reality points to two central roots of suffering in this world: The exercise of free will through which the human condition is changed, and the structure of created reality or creation itself.

Suffering Originating from Human Sources

Human beings are endowed with a free will. This means that the individual is called to constructively live life within the unique limitations of his or her being. This task and purpose of life has been built into humanity by the Creator. All human beings have received a personal responsibility to fulfill this task. No one can do this for anyone else. To a certain extent this task must be sought by each individual through the discovery and application of singular talents, the circumstances of life, and the needs and demands of the society to which we belong.

In this exploration of the purpose of life, an individual can misread the signs and misjudge the responsibilities, or refuse to respond positively to what the task of life seems to be. In both instances there is an *imbalance caused by human decision*. This imbalance will somehow result in stress or hardship for the individual and for members of the society. Sometimes such hardship is unavoidable, but at other times it can be avoided. However, even if in individual instances suffering caused by humans could have been avoided, in view of the human limitations and given human proneness to self-centeredness, it is, in the reality of life, impossible to expect that all persons will act correctly at all times. It is unavoidable that imbalances arise.

It is an invalid argument to say that God could have created a free human will that could not deviate from the ideal fullness of its task. *Created freedom includes necessarily **the ability** to choose between two opposites.* This ability implies at least the possibility of acting against God's will. Taking into account that human freedom can only be exercised within the parameters of incomplete knowledge and information, a continued perfection (flawlessness) cannot be expected. Greshake says it in these words:

> The concept of a created freedom which should be absolutely free of suffering is basically just as contradictory as that of a triangular circle.
>
> If God created freedom into existence, then this necessarily implies the possibility of suffering.
>
> A person can never isolate him or herself to find a true identity in total independence. The meaning of human life unfolds itself only if the person remains within the pre-established framework of meaning which is opened up to him or her as a creature by the creator.[39]

Thus in many instances human persons are responsible for pain and suffering even though the limitations that seem to cause it are inherent to the human condition.

Suffering Caused by the Structure of Created Reality

Many happenings are totally beyond human control. Diseases and epidemics, earthquakes, floods, and other natural disasters occur independently of human activity. The reasons why all this happens are not known, yet all these events are a source of intense suffering. In the pursuit of an answer it is possible, however, to arrive at an intellectually acceptable understanding without violating the concept of a loving God.

Human experience shows clearly how the whole universe is in a state of development. There is a growth process in which the various forms of life and existence develop into stronger and higher forms or they disappear. The origin of the human spirit was a qualitative leap, but being endowed with a spirit did not take the human out of the cosmic reality. The human remains subject to all cosmic laws.

The highest gift to the human is the ability to direct and to (partly) control his or her life. This human freedom has been prepared by a pre-human developmental process which was haphazard and did not follow a precisely outlined program or plan. Greshake writes:

> Creation—whose goal is creaturely free-dom—right from the outset has the form not of an orderly structure, well-furnished and statistically impeccable, but of an untram-meled and playful movement.[40]

This playful movement intrinsically includes shadow sides such as disintegration, waste, and suffering. Pain and suffering become then a necessary "by-product" of development. (Created) Freedom, is an essential dimension in God's plan "to create the human in the image of God." The human is called to give direction to his or her life, to decide which way to arrange that life, either by accepting the goal God implant-ed in this world (and thus choose a life according to God's intent), or by choosing a life that seeks its fulfillment within the limitations of the material world in which he or she lives. This choice contains pain and suffering because of the tension between the cosmic (material) dimensions of the human who is called to reach beyond the material world into the spiritual realm of the divine.

To become free from (not totally controlled by) this dependence on the cosmic reality is a slow developmental process in which humanity must chart its course within the boundaries of its cosmic existence. Therefore, if God used his omnipotent goodness to abolish all suffering, he would also abolish the human ability to make choices (human freedom).

Humanity would no longer be the image of (a free and self-determining) God and with it the ability to love would be destroyed.[41]

Suffering is thus inherent in the human reality, which in its totality must unfold toward God. This unfolding includes change, discomfort, pain, and suffering. Whether the discomfort of growth and unfolding would have pain and suffering if humanity had not sinned is beyond human knowledge. However, when humanity turns away from its authentic vocation and adheres primarily to a material existence, the growth process becomes an experience of alienation from God with consequent pain and suffering. It is, therefore, because of human sinfulness that suffering ultimately receives its disintegrating nature and endangers human freedom. On the other hand, in the human experience of being obliged to choose between integrating suffering into one's life or rejecting it, pain can lead to a stronger dedication and deeper love.

In this context one may also ask whether perhaps the price for freedom is not too high. Is the power and honor of personal freedom so important that it is worth the suffering and pain connected with it? It appears, however, that questioning the price of freedom is not the real question. If life is lived without faith in God, then indeed pain and suffering could be too high a price to pay for freedom. If, on the other hand, one accepts the loving concern of God, the matter is transformed. God does not want humanity to suffer but to integrate suffering into the totality of life in service of God, for example, by choosing the spiritual values of life as one's ultimate fulfillment. In creation God manifests himself and his love. The slow developmental process of cosmic existence, in which humanity shares, is the creative process of formation and growth from chaotic masses into the fullness of life. It is a process of starting (birth), completing (maturation), and letting go (disintegration) until fullness is reached. Throughout this process God communicates a sharing of his own being to creation and the creatures who experience the pains of created conditions. Thus the suffering creature is never alone, but suffers in union with the creating and calling God. We can summarize this in the following steps:

— God created humanity in his own image.

— Just as God is the source of his own being, so must humanity assume responsibility for its own development and unfolding.

— To be(come) the image of God is not an instantaneous happening but a continuous unfolding that belongs to creative development.

— Pain and suffering belong to the slow and continuous unfolding of the human reality and are part of the creative process.

— Because God is present in the creative process, he is also present in human suffering and suffers with humanity.

According to Greshake:

> God shares in the very suffering of human existence in order to enable the human to overcome it. This means that God himself enters into the suffering of humanity.
>
> Whenever suffering does not derive from or is not further sharpened by sin, but where one's total commitment is toward salvation, peace and joy, there endurance takes on a new quality.[42]

All human pain and suffering eventually passes; what remains is the attitude that carried it. When pain is endured in rebellion and resentment, this attitude will take hold of the individual. When it is endured based upon love and concern for personal integration and interhuman love, the union with God will be deepened. Suffering then becomes a special participation in God's creative and redemptive presence and in the unfolding of the mystery of creation. It becomes a sharing in the life and sanctity of God.

INTEGRATING SUFFERING INTO HUMAN WHOLENESS

The unavoidable nature of human suffering leaves us ultimately with two possible (opposing) choices for personal self-realization. The experience of suffering can result in bitterness with an inherent alienation from self, others, and God, or it can lead to an inner peace that integrates suffering into daily life and fosters personal growth. The Scriptures offer a variety of constructive consequences that can result from the integration of suffering into daily life. These will be discussed in more detail in the next chapter. Here I want to reflect on a few constructive and integrative aspects that flow forth from human theological reasoning on suffering.

Suffering Calls Forth and Deepens Interhuman Concern

It is a basic human tendency to be moved by the suffering of fellow human beings, particularly when they are closely related to us. We step out of our own center into the life of another. We allow our own feelings to be shaped by the condition of another person and thus broaden the ambiance of our life. To become part of the life and happiness of another increases the sense of personal value and importance.

The person who receives the support experiences a personal dependence on the one who cares; however, the patient does not lose his or her sense of dignity as an individual on account of this care. In many instances the patient's sense of personal dignity increases because of the experience of another person's concern and dedication. In this giving and receiving, God's creative and redemptive love takes on a human form.

Thus a growth process takes place in the one who cares as well as in the one who receives care. This process of mutual growth is an explicit manifestation of God's love for humanity, and a direct participation of humanity in the creative and redemptive love of God. Thus suffering becomes an integrative factor in human life and a special form of sharing in the redemptive mission of Christ.

Suffering Offers Us a Sharing in the Redemption of the World

According to St. Paul "the whole creation groans in pain" (Rom. 8:22). Suffering cannot be totally overcome in human earthly existence. It belongs to the process of cosmic unfolding even though we are unable to fathom its deepest reasons. Only the human person can give meaning to the playful haphazardness of the evolutionary process. When human beings do not strike back, suffering can become a productive element that places unavoidable material conditions at the service of the goal orientation of cosmic development. Thus the seemingly negative experience of suffering can be transformed into a constructive growth process.

For the believer this often happens in prayer. It then becomes a recognition of dependence on the highest power that gives origin and goal to human existence. Suffering brings us into God's presence and invites us to share in the unfolding of creation, leading humanity to new life guided by the Spirit of God.

Suffering Leads to Interhuman Solidarity

Earlier I have mentioned how suffering leads to human interdependence and thus participates in the creative presence of God. On the purely human level, too, it takes away the hopelessness of the human condition and nurtures human development. This is perhaps best expressed by Greshake when he says:

People who never endured distress have never lived. Those who are covered with wounds now healed, have a special warmth. They have learned that wounds are an examination or test of life, to probe our strength, our innermost convictions, our personal character.[43]

What is true for the individual is also true for society. Dorothy Soelle writes:

One wonders what will become of a society in which certain forms of suffering are avoided gratuitously ... in which a marriage that is perceived as unbearable quickly and smoothly ends in divorce; after divorce, no scars remain; relationships between generations are dissolved as quickly as possible, without a struggle, without a trace; periods of mourning are "sensibly" short; with haste the handicapped and sick are removed from the house and the dead from the mind. If changing marriage partners happens as readily as trading in an old car for a new one, then the experiences that one had in the unsuccessful relationship remain unproductive. From suffering nothing is learned and nothing is to be learned.[44]

Suffering presents itself as a school for human development and personal growth in which the purpose of creation is not only not frustrated but is realized, inviting humanity to share in this creative development and the creative and redemptive self-manifestation of God.

The Christian
community is called
to care for the sick
and suffering as a
participation in the
unfolding of human
life and the full real-
ization of Christ's
redemptive mission.

CHAPTER SIX

The Christian Community:
Concern for the Sick

In Chapter Two I described the Church as "a community of believers who are called and united to make the life and the love of Christ a visible reality on earth."

Christ described the reason for his coming "... that they may have life and have it to the full" (Jn. 10:10). He came to bring a form of wholeness in which human existence on earth would incorporate an intimate relationship to God. In other words, Christ brought a wholeness so that the material and psychological conditions of human life would be integrated with the spiritual vocation of individual and society. Christ conveyed this mission to the Church, therefore the Church shares in this same function, and as a community of believers, she has become a prime resource for health care ministry. To reiterate:

> The Church is the place in which this vision of wholeness must be intensely understood and lived, because the Church is called to be the visibility of Christ in the human community.

In order to understand the healing mission of the Church in today's world we need to study three closely related dynamics: (1) healing in the mission of Christ, (2) how this healing mission is passed on to the Church, and (3) the call to healing in our contemporary society.

HEALING IN THE MISSION OF CHRIST [45]

Christ came to reconcile humanity with the Father. His task was to bring redemption and salvation. He did not come to establish any material kingdom or to change the material setting and surrounding of humanity. He came to reveal the deepest meaning of human existence in its earthly setting. "I will announce what has lain hidden from the foundation of the world" (Mt. 13:35).

Salvation is here understood as "the divine action of deliverance from (the spiritual) evils that afflict human existence." In historical religions such as Judaism and Christianity salvation means: the experience of the divine action in human history, or rather, Christ's presence in the lives of his original followers and in the lives of their successors in the faith.

The actions of Jesus must be seen in the totality of his mission of salvation. His teaching and in particular his healing activity may not be separated from his salvific intentions and mission. This vision of totality becomes especially important for the understanding of the miracles of healing. If these miracles are understood primarily as expressions of compassion with human suffering, and if they are, first of all, a relief from human misery, then Jesus becomes a "miracle worker," and the sick become objects of compassion. Jesus, however, is more than a miracle worker, and those who were healed were more than objects. They were participants in the mystery of salvation.

The miracles of healing are not individual actions of compassion; *they manifest the saving mission of Christ*. They are not merely signs to publicize or underscore a point of teaching, but belong to the message of salvation. Miracles are the visibility of the message, not simply a demonstration of power or a proof for a point of doctrine. Their full meaning does not lie in the miraculous nature of the event, but in the underlying message manifested in the miraculous happenings. The miracles that Jesus performed were never an end in themselves. They pointed to a deeper meaning based always on the element of faith, or the call to believe in the mission of Jesus. This call for faith is expressed in the various undercurrents that give a special meaning to the miraculous events. Briefly, the following discussion highlights four of the most important undercurrents expressing this call for faith.

1. *The value of interhuman relationships* is strongly emphasized in miracles such as the healing of the lepers described in Mt. 8:3; Mk. 1:40–44; and Lk. 5:12 and 17:11–17. Leprosy was more than a physical disease; it was also a social stigma that rendered the afflicted outcasts of society. In healing them, Jesus not only restored their physical integrity, but more importantly, he gave them a personal wholeness restoring them to a state of human dignity. He made the *person* whole not just the body.

   A similar interhuman concern is displayed in the cure of Peter's mother-in-law. In the Jewish community hospitality was one of the major virtues. He restored to her the ability to respond to this social expectation in a normal human way.

   In the miracles of calling back to life Jairus's daughter (Mk. 5:21–43; Lk.8:40–56), the son of the widow of Naim (Lk. 7:11–17), and his friend, Lazarus (Jn. 11:1–44), Jesus responded to deep human concerns. He restored a human wholeness that transcends the external benefit to individuals. Such miracles were to draw the attention of his followers to God's presence in human relationships.

2. *An individual's relationship to God*, particularly the forgiveness of sins, is clearly expressed in the cure of the paralyzed man who had been sick for thirty-eight years. Jesus said to him: "Remember, now, you have been cured. Give up your sins so that something worse may not overtake you" (Jn. 5:14). He gave a similar warning to the paralytic who was let down through the roof (Mk. 2:6). He forgave the person's sins, praised the faith of those who brought him, and confirmed the divine origin of his own mission.

   On several occasions he showed how faith in his mission was a source of wholeness. This is manifest in the cure of the centurion's servant (Mt. 8:5 ff), the woman who suffered from hemorrhaging (Mt. 9:22), and in the restoration of vision to the blind man in Jericho (Mk. 10:52). In these instances he does not refer to forgiveness of sins, but tells them how faith in his mission, faith in God, has been their source of wholeness.

The frequent expulsion of evil spirits points in the same direction. It was the restoration of the ability to relate to God and to live a life of human dignity. In all circumstances Jesus' miracles were the visible manifestation of his mission to restore the human relationship with God.

3. *Human needs have precedence over ritual prescriptions.* The principal teaching in these miracles is that the worship of God is not achieved through a mechanical observance of rites and commandments. Jesus healed the crippled woman on the sabbath to emphasize that the response to the needs of people is more important than ritual observance. In the case of the man with the withered hand, he asked his opponents explicitly: "...is it lawful to do good on the sabbath or evil?" (Lk. 6:9). He wanted to underscore the importance of human concern as a special form of service and worship to God.

4. *Human interchange or the faith of the community* is another element that enters into the understanding of healing. In his own hometown Jesus could not perform miracles because of the unbelief of the people. He stated that a prophet is not without honor except in his own country. These circumstances suggest that healing is not only an act of generosity on the part of God. *Humanity is drawn into the process.* The human requirement that is needed is an interhuman relationship of understanding, concern, and involvement, together with trust and receptivity. The miracles of healing reflect the necessity of an openness to God and of a personal willingness to respond to God's call.

THE MISSION OF HEALING IS PASSED ON TO THE CHURCH

On various occasions Jesus shared his mission with his disciples. He wanted them to prepare people in villages and towns for his coming. He sent seventy-two of his disciples in pairs of two (Lk. 10:1–16) and, on another occasion, his twelve closest friends on a similar mission (Mt. 10:1–16; Mk. 6:7–13; Lk. 9:1–9). Whenever these messengers went out to prepare his coming, he gave them the power to heal the sick and expel demons. Mark tells that they even brought physical alleviation (and human wholeness) by (ritually) anointing the sick with oil. After the resurrection, he commissioned his disciples to bring his teaching to the ends of the earth, and this included the power to heal. The disciples exercised this power as we know from the Acts of the Apostles, for example, Acts 3:6. St. Paul mentions the power of healing among the gifts of the Spirit for the good of the community (1 Cor. 12:9 and 28). The power of healing is the living sign of the loving presence of God among believers. At no point is the power of healing an end in itself. Without the actual concern for the sick, the message of Christ seems to be incomplete. The miracles of healing that were performed in the early Church were simultaneously an expression of compassion and an instruction in the understanding of Christ's message.

This element of Christian formation indicates a second aspect of the total meaning of the mission of healing: *it must bring to the community an understanding and a sensitivity that everyone carries a share in reaching out for the well-being and the wholeness of all.* This reaching out is prominently manifested in the concern for the sick. The helplessness of the sick, their inability to care for themselves, their dependence on the care of others, are visible reflections of the human condition of total dependence on God. The care for those in need translates into human visibility the constant presence of God's creative and redemptive love. It is the task of the Church to bring this mentality and generosity to life in all believers.

The apostolic Church practiced what Jesus had taught. The apostles' concern for people in need was the reason why they appointed the first deacons in the Church (Acts 6:1–7). By doing so, a special ministry of concern for the needs of others became a visible expression of God's concern for the dignity of all. It was also a ministry that included an essential involvement of the community, who chose the first deacons, and a recognition of this ministry by the authorities.

The early Church did not institute any organized system of caring for the sick. This task was completely incorporated in the community and manifested itself in the actions of individuals. There is no doubt that in their mind the healing mission was an inseparable part of the mandate that Jesus had given them.

During subsequent centuries the mission of healing was less frequently expressed in "miraculous" cures. This does not mean that it had lost its importance. Rather, it indicates that the healing mission itself as a visible manifestation of the mission of salvation and redemption was in a different stage of development. It had become part of the Christian heritage. The rise of persons such as St. Elizabeth of Hungary (b. 1207), St. Vincent de Paul (b. 1581), St. Camillus de Lellis (b. 1582), and St. Louise de Marillac (b. 1591) is a living testimony of the Church's concern for the sick and the suffering. When this care became too demanding for individual endeavors, they led the community into more organized forms of health care apostolate.

The rise of these persons indicates a shift in the Church's understanding of the mission of healing. Their activity was both a personal concern for those who suffer and an effort to bring the concern for the sick to the attention of the community at large. They pointed to the task of the Christian community to participate in the mission of healing, not merely by bringing consolation to those in suffering, but by utilizing their own possessions and talents for the support of the needy. They created places where professionalism and compassion blended into one expression of human involvement.

This brings us to our third point: understanding the mission of healing in our modern society.

THE CALL TO HEALING
IN CONTEMPORARY SOCIETY

One of the principal teachings of Vatican Council II is the new vision on the People of God in which all, laity and hierarchy, are mutually interdependent but also have their own responsibilities. The community as a whole is called to live/express in their daily lives the reality of God's presence. All are participants in creation and redemption; no category consists of merely recipients. The Constitution on the Church in the Modern World points to this task:

> By the work of his hands and with the aid of technical means the human person tills the earth to bring forth fruit and to make it a dwelling place fit for all mankind; the individual also consciously plays his/her part in the life of social groups; in so doing he/she realizes the design which God revealed at the beginning of time, to subdue the earth and perfect the work of creation, and at the same time they improve their own person. They also observe the command of Christ to devote themselves to the service of their fellow human beings (GS 57).[46]

If we define salvation as "the divine action of deliverance from evils that afflict human existence" then salvation must extend itself to all creation. St. Paul indicates the extent of salvation when he says: "…we know that all creation groans and is in agony even until now. Not only that, but we ourselves, although we have the Spirit as first fruits, groan inwardly while we await the redemption of our bodies" (Rom. 8:22–23). Redemption is more than a concern for the spiritual aspects of human life. It is a concern for wholeness in human existence on earth.

It is the role of the Christian community, especially lay people, to bring about this integration of spiritual values into the material setting of this world. Vatican Council II teaches this in these words:

> The characteristic of the lay state being a life led in the midst of the world and of worldly affairs, lay people are called by God to make of their apostolate, through the vigor of their Christian spirit, a leaven in the world (AA 2).[47]

This involvement in material affairs needs to be: (1) a contribution to the unfolding of material existence and (2) a leaven for the wholeness of the human community in its task to make material existence a clearer manifestation of God's presence. The progress of science, particularly medical technology, places this task of the lay person in a special light.

Human beings in our culture are strongly inclined to get so wrapped up in external and scientific developments that there is little or no room left for religious values. Scientific research is also very reluctant to attribute to an invisible cause what one can see and touch. Consequently, in progressive scientific involvement it is difficult to retain a vision of God's active and creative presence, when visible solutions seem to be at hand.

The Church has a task in this world of science. Faith does not increase human technical abilities, but places them in a special perspective. It integrates them with the invisible and spiritual realities indispensable for human life and wholeness.

The material world must be integrated into the saving action of Christ by acknowledging that all scientific progress is a dimension of God's self-revelation and a participation in God's creative plan. In other words, it is the Church's task to fill all material existence with God's saving love, and to carry out this salvific plan in her own actions and involvement. This responsibility must be applied also to the Church's concern for the sick. Harry Gielen describes this task as follows:

> The healing mission of the Church is not called to create a religious alternative to science. The Church

is called to acknowledge God's active presence that reveals itself in every new discovery. It is a Christian mandate to bring about in mankind an attitude of openness to the Spirit, so that more people may recognize God's actions at the place where they live, namely, in our contemporary world which, despite its limitations and tragedies, is still the place where God gives his Son to us.

Christians are called to be a leaven in this world through their contribution to professionalism, through loving service to the neighbor, and through relationships with colleagues and patients.

They are called to be this leaven in the conviction that God is present and alive in our time. Activities that otherwise would remain purely technical, distant and cold, will then be activities that in obedience and dedication to God become a self-manifestation of the one who gave his life for his friends.[48]

This task of integration rests primarily on the hospital as institution through its administration and medical personnel. It remains, however, the mandate of the Church to inspire this spirit of "salvific" healing in those who dedicate themselves to the healing profession. Where this integration does not take place, there is a danger that patients will be reduced to objects at the service of medical knowledge and technology. In this process they may lose their dignity as persons. D. Emeis explains this:[49]

The loss of human dignity (in hospitals) is not only felt in the fact the sick feel themselves separated from society, the healthy also suffer because of the lack of contact with the sick. They cannot learn from those who suffer, and they cannot be available to the sick or prepare themselves for personal sickness. A society that does not isolate its sick and that does not exclude hospitals from its residential areas, shows more respect for human dignity than a society that entrusts its sick to institutions with which it has no other contact than financial transactions (p.119).

There are many hospitals in which illness is simply not accepted as a participation in a human or Christian mandate. The only people who seem to have a task in the hospital are the physicians and other health care professionals. The patients are there only to be treated. That the patients themselves are at that moment faced with a task which is perhaps the most serious task of their life, is overlooked ...(p.121).

A Christian hospital is a place where physicians and other health care professionals relate to the patients in such a way that they (the patients) will experience their illness as a stage in life which they live in partnership with God (p.122).

The patients' task in the hospital is twofold: (1) To take the best possible steps to overcome (cure or stabilize) the illness that prevents effective self-expression and (2) To integrate their present condition into the wholeness of their life as it is at this moment of their existence.

In view of this mandate for integration, the Church cannot limit its pastoral concern for the sick to their spiritual care only. Emeis expresses this as follows:

Pastoral care in a hospital is not only the spiritual care for the sick, it includes also our communal care for one another and for our Christian identity (p.122).

Elsewhere I have described this responsibility in these words:

> If the Church limits the main thrust of its mission of healing to the spiritual care of those who are sick, without making very serious efforts for the integration of spiritual values into medical, scientific and technological development, then the Church herself would be guilty of creating and promoting a separation of values which is in direct contradiction to the message of the Gospel as it is interpreted in Vatican Council II.[50]

The Church as a Christian community and as the People of God is called to live the fullness of Christ's life. This fullness of life is not completely realized in feelings of concern and compassion. It must be translated into everyday activity. Christianity is not merely a message; it is a principle of living and a principle of truth. This truth can communicate itself only through life, in the integration of spiritual values in human daily activities.

The responsibility of the Christian community in the concern for the sick rests on firmly interlocking principles:

1. The mission of healing that Jesus entrusted to the Church is not fulfilled solely in the spiritual care and consolation of the sick. The Church must also convey the responsibility for this mission of healing to all who are involved in the distribution of health care.

2. The Christian community, which received the mandate of healing from Christ himself, must be the leaven of the community at large so that in medical professionalism the saving and healing love of God can become visible. The hospital is the proper place for this involvement.

Jesus passed on to his Church not only the miraculous power of healing, but the mandate to bring wholeness to individuals and society. Miraculous healings are but an external manifestation of the underlying mandate. The spiritual care of the sick is one part of its fulfillment. The Christian community is called to care for the sick and suffering as a participation in the unfolding and sanctification of human life and the full realization of Christ's redemptive mission.

NOTES

Chapter One
1. A more extensive discussion of this topic can be found in Cornelius van der Poel, *The Search for Human Values* (New York: Paulist Press, 1972), 11–72.

Chapter Two
2. "Change in the Church," *The New Catholic Encyclopedia*, vol. 17, supplement (Washington D.C., 1979), 118.

3. *Vatican Council II: The Conciliar and Post Conciliar Documents*, ed. Austin Flannery, O.P. (North Port, New York: Costello Publishing Company, 1981), 350 ff.

4. Ibid., 352–54.

5. Christopher Butler, *The Theology of Vatican II* (London: Darton, Longman & Todd, 1962), 60.

6. Ibid., 63.

7. *The New Catholic Encyclopedia*, 537.

8. These concepts are discussed in more detail by Richard McBrien in "The Catholic Church: Relevance and Mission," *Hospital Progress* (January 1973), 84–89.

Chapter Three
9. Antonellus Elsasser, "Gesundheit und Krankeit," *Stimmen der Zeit* (June 1982), 373–84.

10. See "Managing Pain," *Mayo Clinic Health Letter*, supplement (June 1996), 2.

11. Ibid., 1.

12. Theodore Bovet, "Human Attitudes Toward Suffering," *Humanities* 9, no. 1 (Pittsburgh, Pennsylvania:

Institute of Man, Duquesne University) 5–20. Reprinted in *The Meaning of Human Suffering,* (Notre Dame, Indiana: University of Notre Dame Press, 1979).

13. Dorothy Soelle, "Suffering and Language,"*Suffering* (Philadelphia: Fortress Press, 1975), 69.

14. Robert Goldenson, *Encyclopedia of Human Behavior* 1 (Garden City, New York: Doubleday, 1970), 314.

15. A useful description, within the comprehension of "lay-persons," is given in the Medical Essay, supplement to the *Mayo Clinic Health Letter,* October, 1998.

16. *Diagnostic and Statistical Manual of Mental Disorders,* 4th edition, 300.40 (American Psychiatric Association, 1994), 349.

17. Soelle, *Suffering,* 70–74.

18. Quoted in Bovet, "Human Attitudes."

19. See J. William Worden, *Grief Counseling and Grief Therapy: A Handbook for the Mental Health Practitioner* (New York: Springer Publishing Co., 1991), 7–8.

20. Ibid., 9–19.

21. Lynne Ann DeSpelder and Albert Strickland, *The Last Dance: Encountering Death and Dying* (Palo Alto, California: Mayfield Publishing Company, 1983), 193.

22. Quoted in Bovet, "Human Attitudes."

23. Erich Lindemann, "Symtomology and Management of Acute Grief," in *Understanding Death and Dying,* Sandra Galdieri Wilcox and Marilyn Sutton (Palo Alto,

California: Mayfield Publishing Company, 1981), 148.

24. Wilcox and Sutton, 154.

25. Theresa Rando, *Grief, Dying and Death: Clinical Interventions for Caregivers* (Research Press Company, 1984), 43 ff.

26. Dr. Wayne E. Oates, *Forms of Grief, Diagnosis, Meaning, and Treatment,* in *The Meaning of Human Suffering,* Presentations of the First International Congress on the Meaning of Human Suffering, ed. Flavian Dougherty (New York: Human Science Press, 1982), 232–65.

27. Elizabeth Kuebler-Ross, *On Death and Dying,* (New York: MacMillan Publishing Company, 1969), 11 ff.

Chapter Four

28. For a brief description of such theories, one can consult *Man, Myth and Magic: An Encyclopedia of the Supernatural* 7, ed. Richard Cavendish (New York: Marshal Cavendish Corporation, 1970), 858–64.

29. Ibid., 860–61.

30. Many of the thoughts in this section are taken from or inspired by Caroll Stuhlmueller's "Voices of Suffering in Biblical Prophecy and Prayer," in *The Meaning of Human Suffering,* 97 ff.

31. For the biblical references in this section I have made extensive use of *Sacramentum Verbi* 3, ed. J.B. Bauer (New York: Herder & Herder, 1970), 890 ff.

32. See Jos Luyten, "Perspectives on Human Suffering in the Old Testament," in *God and Human Suffering,* Louvain Theological Pastoral Monographs, eds. Jan Lambrecht

and Raymond Collins (Grand Rapids, Michigan: Eerdmans, 1990), 1–30.

33. See Lambrecht and Collins, "Paul and Suffering," *God and Human Suffering,* 47–68.

34. See Robrecht Michiels, "Jesus and Suffering: The Suffering of Jesus," in Lambrecht and Collins, *God and Human Suffering,* 31–46.

35. Arthur McGill, "Human Suffering and the Passion of Christ," in Lambrecht and Collins, *God and Human Suffering,* 172 ff.

Chapter Five

36. Gisbert Greshake, "Human Suffering and the Question of God," *Stauros Bulletin* 1 (Leuven, Belgium: Stauros International Association, 1977), 21.

37. Edward Schillebeeckx, "The Mystery of Injustice and the Mystery of Mercy," *Stauros Bulletin* 3 (Leuven, Belgium: Stauros International Association, 1975).

38. Ibid., 19–20.

39. Ibid., 25–26.

40. Ibid., 30.

41. Ibid., 31.

42. Ibid., 20, 34.

43. Ibid., 40.

44. Soelle, *Suffering,* 38.

Chapter Six

45. David Stanley, "Salvation and Healing," in *The Way* (1970), 298–313.

46. The Pastoral Constitution on the Church in the Modern World *(Gaudium et spes)* in *Vatican Council II: The Conciliar and Post Conciliar Documents*, 961.

47. The Decree on the Apostolate of Lay People *(Apostolicam actuositatem)*, in *Vatican Council II: The Conciliar and Post Conciliar Documents*, 768.

48. Harry Gielen, "Christelijke Zielzorg en Pastoraat" (Christian Care of Souls and Pastoral Care), *Pastorale Gids voor Verzorgings Instellingen*, Part I, Section A, Article 2, page 1.

49. D. Emeis, "Was ist ein Christliche Krankenhaus?" (What is a Christian Hospital?), *Stimmen der Zeit* (1976), 117–126.

50. Cornelius van der Poel, *The Mission of Healing: A Mandate of the Church* (Columbus, Ohio: Dominican Sisters, 1982), 32.

INDEX

A
Aquinas, St. Thomas 3
attachment 56

B
Bible
    see also *pain and suffering*
    pain and suffering in 71–94

body
    role in human life 37–40

Bonhoefer, Dietrich 53

Bovet, Theodore 47

C
Camillus de Lellis, St. 116

Canonical Mission 9

Catholic Action 9

Christian community
    see also *Church*
    and ministry 15–16
    concern for the sick 111–122

Christian life
    see also *Christian community*
    is kingly 21
    is priestly 20
    is prophetic 21

Church
    as communion 28–29
    as community of believers 16–26
    as community called to
        holiness 22–23
    as community of people 15
    as grace-filled organization 16–19
    as grace-giving human
        interaction 19–22
    as herald 30
    as institution 27–28
    as sacrament 29–30
    as servant 31
    as structured community 27–31
    called to manifest God's presence in
        the world 23–25

concern for the sick 111–122
healing mission of 111–122
health care as mandate to 15–33
models of 27–31
nature of 18
role and characteristics of 25–26
source of health care ministry 32–33
task of salvation 20

Clement, St. 8

Code of Canon Law 9

coping 44

creation
    as interhuman relationship 2
    calls for ministry 1–5
    definition of 2

D
depression 48–50

DeSpelder, Lynne Ann 57

DeVeuster, Fr. Damian 47

drugs 52

Dulles, Avery 27

E
Eckhart, Meister 56

Elizabeth of Hungary, St. 116

Elsasser, Antonellus 40

Emeis, D. 119–120

G
Gielen, Harry 118

Goldenson, Robert 48

Greshake, Gisbert 98, 100–101, 103,
    104, 106, 108

grieving
    see *loss and*

Sheed & Ward

Other Books of Interest
available at your favorite bookstore

Health Care and Information Ethics
Protecting Fundamental Human Rights
ed. Audrey R. Chapman
Major changes are taking place within our health care
system. This volume brings together experts in the field of
information ethics and health care to explore the
implications of these challenges that impact what kind of
care will be available, who especially will receive that care,
and how that care will be monitored. Exploring four
fundamental human rights, universality, privacy,
nondiscrimination, and consent, his book looks honestly at
the complexities and challenges of health care ethics.
P 480 pp 1-55612-922-X *$29.95*

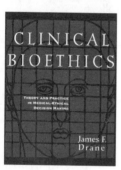

Clinical Bioethics
Theory and Practice in Medical-Ethical Decision Making
James F. Drane
More than ever before, medical practice requires that
medical professionals develop high ethical standards. This
book provides for the busy clinical professional a concise,
comprehensive treatment of the basics in the field of
medical ethics. Including case studies, standards for
patient competency and quality of life, as well as presenting
a general ethics theory and bibliography, *Clinical Bioethics*
will allow you to make informed decisions and take
responsible moral action.
P 300 pp 1-55612-612-3 *$24.95*

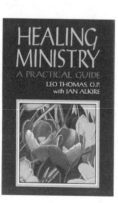

Healing Ministry: A Practical Guide
Leo Thomas, OP
A balanced and practical resource for parish staffs,
prayer groups and individuals who minister to the
sick and suffering. A compassionate book that underscores
the relationship between physical, spiritual and emotional
healing. Concepts of team ministry, a discussion of pastoral
listening, and a theology of sacramentals and spiritual gifts
make this an especially diverse and practical guide for
ministry by Christian caregivers.
P 240 pp 1-55612-673-5 *$12.95*

SHEED & WARD
An Apostolate of the Priests of the Sacred Heart
7373 South Lovers Lane Road
Franklin, Wisconsin 53132

Email sheed@execpc.com *Phone* 1 800 558 0580 or *Fax* 1 800 369 4448